Building a Coaching Culture

Building a Coaching Culture

*The Ripple Effect Raising
Performance and Growth*

Kimberly Lee

BUSINESS EXPERT PRESS

Leader in applied, concise business books

Building a Coaching Culture:
The Ripple Effect Raising Performance and Growth

Copyright © Business Expert Press, LLC, 2026.

Cover design by Jada Simone Haynes

Interior design by S4Carlisle Publishing Services, Chennai, India

First published in 2026 by
Business Expert Press, LLC
222 East 46th Street, New York, NY 10017
www.businessexpertpress.com

ISBN-13: 978-1-63742-942-6 (paperback)
ISBN-13: 978-1-63742-943-3 (e-book)

Human Resource Management and Organizational Behavior Collection

First edition: 2026

10 9 8 7 6 5 4 3 2 1

EU SAFETY REPRESENTATIVE
Mare Nostrum Group B.V.
Mauritskade 21D
1091 GC Amsterdam
The Netherlands
gpsr@mare-nostrum.co.uk

Review Quotes

"Coaching is not a soft, peripheral leadership activity, but one of the most scalable levers for performance, culture, and even innovation. In this book, Kim Lee uses her vast experience to clearly articulate why and how coaching can enable these higher goals, with practical lessons that we can all apply immediately. Building a Coaching Culture: The Ripple Effect Raising Performance and Growth *is a framework for leading differently, with a style of influence that helps others and ourselves approach problem-solving more effectively, not by having the right answers but by modeling the key behaviors that build trust. In doing so, it provides a roadmap for leading with impact through the complex times ahead. A very timely guide."*—**Carlos Larracilla, Cofounder and CEO, Wowledge**

"When burnout outpaces hiring, Building a Coaching Culture *shows that coaching is a manager's strongest tool, pairing repeatable frameworks with hard metrics to retain talent and raise performance."*—**Dr. Milton Mattox, Chief Executive Officer, United States Artificial Intelligence Institute**

"Building a Coaching Culture: The Ripple Effect Raising Performance and Growth *is intuitive, practical, and immediately applicable. The book flows naturally, making coaching concepts easy to grasp and apply. The tools author, Kim Lee, shares are clear, and the insights are highly relatable. The Ripple Effect framework empowers leaders to build trust and elevate performance. A must-read for leaders looking to make a lasting impact."*—**Brian Sherman, EVP, Chief People Officer, Delta Dental of California**

"What I love most about this book is its timely message—it gets to the heart of why so many people are disengaged today and gives leaders a clear path to fix it. Kim's experience is real and her insights have led to an approach that is both refreshing and very actionable."—**Eric S. Walsh Executive Managing Director, MRI Software LLC**

"*Kim Lee's* Building a Coaching Culture *redefines what leadership looks like in the modern workplace—accessible, inclusive, and rooted in belief in human potential. It's both a wake-up call and a guide for leaders ready to create lasting ripple effects.*"—**Dorie Clark,** ***Wall Street Journal*** **&** ***USA Today*** **bestselling author of** ***The Long Game***

Description

In an age of burnout, quiet quitting, and rapid technological change, traditional management is no longer enough. The book, *Building a Coaching Culture: The Ripple Effect Raising Performance and Growth*, offers a powerful, research-backed alternative: a human-centered approach that not only boosts productivity but also transforms people. Author Kim Lee, with decades of leadership experience, introduces "The Ripple Effect"—a unique framework demonstrating how targeted coaching behaviors create waves of positive change that elevate individuals, strengthen company culture, and drive measurable growth.

From a varsity swim team to the boardroom, the principles remain the same. The book shows how investing in people acts as a powerful defense against costly employee turnover, proving that genuine connection and human development are the keys to lasting success. Whether you're a CEO or a first-time manager navigating the complexities of an AI-integrated workplace, this guide provides the tools to:

- Activate talent through powerful coaching conversations.
- Deliver feedback that fuels, not frightens.
- Lead with empathy while driving real results.
- Build a culture of trust, empowerment, and purpose.
- Coach your team through technological change and ambiguity.

This book is a guide for leaders ready to lead with clarity, courage, and a coach's mindset. It shows that you don't need to be a certified coach to create a ripple. You just need to believe that your people are worth it.

Dedication

To my family and friends, especially Trever, whose unwavering belief and endless encouragement provided the foundation for this work. Your support is the true ripple effect in my life.

To my parents: thank you for always being there. Dad, for getting me to swim practice at 5:30 a.m., and Mom, for coming out of retirement to lend your English teacher's eye to this manuscript. I love you both.

To my sons, Justin and Zach: my hope is that this book serves as a small part of my legacy, a reminder that we can all achieve great things.

I am forever grateful to the leaders and mentors who have guided me. A heartfelt thank you to the late Coach Zirzow, who first saw potential in me that I couldn't see in myself. To "New Cool Craig," you taught me the true meaning of human-centered leadership. And to Eric, you are not only a great friend but also my champion and inspiration. Thank you for always having my back.

Finally, to every leader who dares to see the unseen potential in others, who chooses connection over control, and who understands that true success isn't built on tasks but built on the transformative power of human growth. May your ripples create oceans.

Acknowledgments

Creating this book was a ripple effect in itself, and I am deeply grateful to the many individuals who contributed their expertise, encouragement, and belief to bring *Building a Coaching Culture* to life.

My sincere appreciation goes to Enrique Rubio. His insightful foreword not only frames the essence of this book but also serves as a testament to his visionary leadership in the HR space. His dedication to human-centered growth has been a constant inspiration.

To the entire team at Business Expert Press: your guidance, editorial prowess, and commitment to this project were invaluable. Thank you for transforming my manuscript into a polished and impactful work.

I extend heartfelt thanks to Scott Isenberg for his partnership and support throughout the writing and editing process. His belief in a new author made this a truly collaborative journey.

To my early readers and reviewers, especially Erin McCarthy, Craig Lyon, Randi McKenna, and Jess Morenko, your candid feedback and insightful questions helped shape and refine every chapter. Your perspectives were truly critical. A special thanks to my niece, Jada Simone Haynes, for her beautiful book cover art.

Finally, to my family and friends, thank you for your patience and unwavering belief in this endeavor. Your love and encouragement were the silent forces that kept me going, especially on the days when the words wouldn't flow. This book is a reflection of many minds and hearts, and I am deeply thankful for each ripple that contributed to its creation.

Contents

Foreword

As I was starting my career, and even as I grew into a midlevel leadership role, there was one thing that always puzzled me: Coaching was treated like a luxury. Something reserved for executives. A perk at the top. In full transparency, it bothered me.

And while those at the highest levels were given coaches to refine their leadership, the rest of us, the frontline leaders, the emerging managers, the high-potentials in the middle, all of us were left to figure it out on our own.

What I saw back then and what this book captures with precision and power is that we weren't just creating unequal access to development, but we were missing a massive opportunity. We were intentionally and by design relinquishing the chance to build strong, scalable leadership pipelines, slowing the potential of our organizations and, ultimately, creating cultures where performance relied too heavily on positional authority instead of shared growth.

More than that, we were losing something even bigger: the chance to create a ripple effect.

That's the beating heart of *Building a Coaching Culture: The Ripple Effect Raising Performance and Growth.*

As my friend and HR leader extraordinaire Kim Lee so beautifully defines it, the ripple effect is *"a coaching action that creates a significant and expanding impact beyond the original conversation or relationship."*

The ripple effect is what happens when coaching doesn't stay trapped in a 1:1 meeting between a leader and their coach, particularly senior leaders, but what becomes part of how people interact every day with their peers and teams: listening, supporting, challenging, and growing together. The ripple effect expands beyond the individual and impacts culture, all around, which, simultaneously, impacts the bottom line and goals of an organization.

The best part? This ripple doesn't start with a mandate or a million-dollar program. It starts with one person choosing to lead differently.

Building a Coaching Culture: The Ripple Effect Raising Performance and Growth is both a manifesto and a practical guide for that kind of leadership. It challenges us to move away from the idea that coaching is something external or something someone else does to improve our performance. The book makes the case that coaching is also internal: a way of being; a way of showing up in our roles, our conversations, and our choices with greater intention, empathy, and belief in human potential. And Kim maps this out with clarity and depth.

Across the chapters, you'll discover how coaching culture is about skill-building and system design and integrating coaching into how we hire, onboard, develop, promote, and lead.

In *Building a Coaching Culture: The Ripple Effect Raising Performance and Growth*, you'll explore how psychological safety, feedback loops, listening practices, and talent mobility, all contribute to a culture where people coach each other.

One of the most powerful threads in this book is the emphasis on access and equity. We cannot call ourselves people-first leaders if coaching is only available to the few, like it happened to me for most of the beginning of my career. When we democratize coaching and we make it part of the everyday fabric of team life and organizational culture, we end up unlocking performance at scale. We make development inclusive and available. And we send a clear message to every employee: Growth is not exclusive. It's expected. It's supported. And it's shared.

Kim brings this to life with research and relatable stories of managers who went from task-focused to people-focused; of teams that became more connected, more creative, and more capable because someone chose to listen differently; of employees who felt seen and valued in ways that reshaped their trajectory.

But perhaps the most timely and urgent message of *Building a Coaching Culture* is found in the chapter: coaching in the age of AI.

As someone who has spent years working at the intersection of HR, leadership, and technology (including artificial intelligence), I can say this with conviction: The organizations that will thrive in the coming years are not the ones with the most advanced tech, as much of a competitive advantage as that is, but the ones that know how to stay human as they adopt and integrate it.

AI is transforming how we work, but coaching is one of the core human capabilities that will remain deeply relevant and determine how we grow. Kim makes this point with nuance and power. She shows that

AI doesn't erase the need for coaching but amplifies it. When technology handles more of the repetitive and mundane tasks, we are freed up to focus on what only humans can do: solve complex problems, build meaningful connections, think creatively, and, well, creating people-first ripple effects by supporting one another's growth.

This is where the four "Cs" that Kim outlines—complex problemsolving; connection; creativity; and coaching itself—become phenomenal organizational opportunities. They are the traits that define great teams, great cultures, and great leaders in the age of automation.

The ripple effect, in this new digital era, becomes even more vital. A leader who models ethical AI usage sparks a conversation. That conversation becomes an opportunity for innovation. That innovation turns into a new strategy that requires a new policy. That policy becomes a new standard. That standard shapes how people work, build, and collaborate. The ripple grows, within coaching and beyond it.

In a world where fear of AI can spread just as fast as the advancement of AI itself, this kind of positive ripple is essential. Kim reminds us that the role of futuristic, people-first leaders is to guide people through uncertainty with presence, clarity, and courage.

That's what this book is: a guide to building a coaching culture, a reminder that we are the culture and that every conversation is a chance to shift the system and our own mindsets. This book shows us that every act of coaching, whether it's a question asked, a truth told with compassion, or a moment of silence held in empathy, can create impact far beyond what we see.

So whether you're an HR professional designing programs, a team leader navigating hybrid work, a CEO rethinking your org structure, or a first-time manager trying to do right by your team, this book is for you.

It will challenge you. It will equip you. And, if you let it, it will create ripples from and through you.

As Kim Lee so clearly shows us, when we choose to lead as coaches, not just once, but always, we change people and culture, and, ultimately, everything in life and work, and in between.

And that changes everything.

Enrique Rubio, Founder and CEO, Hacking HR

Author's Note: Leading with Empathy, Intuition, and a Dash of Reality

Maybe you picked up this book thinking, "Another leadership guide? What's this one going to teach me that I haven't heard in a TED Talk?" Fair question. The shelves are full of strategy manuals and success blueprints. And yes—we'll absolutely unpack proven frameworks and compelling research. But this isn't just another textbook.

My path into leadership wasn't mapped out—it meandered through unexpected turns, including a brief chapter as a competitive swimmer (spoiler: the pool taught me more about resilience than any boardroom). What's guided me all along is an instinctive drive to notice what others overlook—the quiet potential, the untapped brilliance, the moment someone just needs one person to believe in them.

My style blends deep intuition, empathetic listening, and a steady impulse to spark meaningful change—because sometimes, the person rewriting the rules isn't the loudest in the room, just the one paying closest attention.

Leadership, as I've come to learn, isn't a highlight reel. It's often a patchwork of late-night reflections, gut calls, and small courageous moments no one claps for. This book is a companion for leaders who know connection is the real ROI and that nurturing people isn't a soft skill—it's the job.

Together, we'll explore how to lead with both heart and backbone—leveraging not just what you do but also who you are. Because let's be honest: The best leadership often begins with seeing possibility in others before they do, and, sometimes, navigating the messy brilliance of human potential takes a strong cup of coffee and a sense of humor. People aren't formulas—and that's the beautiful part.

Introduction: The Ripple You Create

Today's workplace is a dynamic, ever-evolving landscape, and it's clear that traditional management styles are struggling to keep pace. Many leaders find themselves facing common challenges: employees feeling disengaged, productivity stalling, and valuable talent moving on. *A ResumeTemplates. com survey of 1,258 full-time U.S. workers in October 2024 found that 56% of them plan to look for a new job in 2025. Of those workers, 27% were already actively looking for a new job. Additionally, the survey found that one in three job seekers are willing to quit their current job even if they don't have another one lined up. The top reasons for this were low pay (40% of respondents), feeling undervalued (37%), and burnout (37%). Work-life balance was the most important factor for job seekers, with 99% of respondents considering it a key priority.* Simply directing tasks and checking off boxes just isn't enough anymore; it can actually hold teams back and miss out on incredible potential.

But what if there was a different path? What if your team meetings weren't just scheduled time but instead are vibrant hubs of genuine collaboration and spontaneous breakthroughs? What if every feedback session left your people not just understanding more but, more importantly, *feeling more energized* and more deeply connected to their purpose? Imagine a world where employees don't just show up; they *thrive*, where their hidden strengths aren't just acknowledged but actively *unlocked*. A more human-centered yet strategically powerful approach that could truly unlock your team's hidden strengths, significantly boost your organization's success, and cultivate a deeply inspired and committed workforce?

This book is built on a simple but powerful premise: Your leadership is a ripple. Every conversation, piece of feedback, and question you ask sends waves of influence through your team and organization. The only choice is what kind of ripple you will create. This book is your guide to making it one of courage, connection, and growth.

This isn't about fleeting fads or so-called soft skills that don't deliver; it's about embracing the transformative power of coaching. My journey into this philosophy began unexpectedly during my freshman year when I joined the competitive swim team with no experience. My coach saw a potential in me that I couldn't see in myself. He refined my technique and gave me the confidence needed to compete, and soon, I was winning races. That experience ignited a lifelong belief: Coaching isn't just about technique. It's about seeing what's possible in others and nurturing their potential until they can see it too. This is the heart of the "ripple effect"—a force for positive change that can transform individuals, teams, and entire organizations.

What Makes This Book Different? A Framework for Real-World Leadership

The coaching shelf is crowded. So, what makes this book stand out? It's built on a three-part framework designed not for a theoretical world but instead for the messy reality of the modern workplace.

1. The "Ripple Effect" Model: We move beyond one-off coaching interactions to explore a systemic truth: Small, consistent coaching behaviors create cascading waves of positive change. When you coach one person effectively, you are not just developing an individual; you are modeling a behavior that they, in turn, will use with their peers, creating a self-sustaining culture of growth that spreads organically. This is the what: the exponential, cultural impact of coaching.

2. The HR Leader's Lens: This book is written with the perspective of an HR leader—a view that's as ground-level and observant as a coach's on the pool deck. Unlike a CEO viewing the organization from afar or a consultant from the outside, an HR leader has a unique, systemic view of the entire employee lifecycle. This perspective provides a practical, systemic playbook for embedding coaching into the real-world architecture of your company—from hiring and onboarding to performance management, conflict resolution, and even respectful exits. This is the how: the practical guide to building the cultural infrastructure for coaching to thrive.

3. A Tactical Focus on Inflection Points: We will focus on the moments where leadership matters most. While many books address steady-state management, this one provides a playbook for navigating the inflection points—the moments of volatility and change where a coach's guidance is most critical. We explore how to use coaching as your most essential tool during the critical "inflection points" of organizational life—mergers and acquisitions, major re-orgs, technological disruptions like AI, and the personal career breakthroughs and breakdowns that define an employee's journey. This is the when: a tactical guide for leading through uncertainty.

This integrated approach—exploring the what, the how, and the when—is what makes *Coaching Culture: The Ripple Effect* a distinct and indispensable guide for today's leader.

This book is your invitation to start creating your own.

CHAPTER 1

The Coaching Mindset— Lessons from the Field and Beyond

The vision of a truly engaged and empowered workplace is compelling, isn't it? But before we dive into the data and the how-to, it's important to understand *why* this isn't just theory for me. An understanding of the impact of coaching can develop through real-life experiences, such as observing effective mentorship in settings like a high school swimming pool, where its influence first becomes evident.

My belief in the transformative power of coaching isn't theoretical; it was forged in the chlorine-scented air of a high school swimming pool. My journey began my freshman year when, with absolutely no experience, I decided to try out for the swim team. I somehow made varsity, specializing in the grueling butterfly stroke. But what still amazes me is not just that I made the team; it's that I started winning races almost immediately.

I attribute this remarkable feat to my coach, Coach Zirzow. He was tough but fair, with an uncanny ability to see a strength in me I didn't know I had. I can still hear his voice echoing across the water, yelling my last name, pushing me to refine my technique. He ignited a passion in me so intense that I started practicing twice a day—once at 5 a.m. (thanks for getting me there each morning, Dad!) and again after school. His coaching didn't just help me excel; it taught me a lesson that has shaped my entire career. It showed me the significant impact a leader can have by truly seeing someone's potential and helping them unlock it, regardless of their starting point.

Though I didn't realize it at the time, that experience fundamentally shaped my view of leadership. Coach Zirzow taught me that coaching isn't about pointing out flaws; it's about seeing potential and helping people discover it for themselves. This is the first, most critical action that creates what I call the "ripple effect": the understanding that stronger, more capable individuals naturally build stronger, more successful teams.

When coaching becomes central to how a team works, the effect is transformative. Communication improves, motivation deepens, and the entire organization becomes more agile. This is where the ripple truly begins to spread: Individuals who are coached well are often inspired to coach others, creating a self-sustaining culture of growth.

My coaching journey started in a pool, but the principles quickly translated to other arenas. As a longtime football fan—and a mom who spent nearly a decade in the stands watching my son's practices and games—it became clear that every team has a unique culture, and the coach is its primary architect.

Let's consider two legendary NFL coaches who exemplify diverse yet highly effective coaching styles: Bill Belichick and Andy Reid. They highlight different, though equally valid, paths to building a championship-caliber organization.

Bill Belichick: The "Do Your Job" Architect

Think about the Patriots' culture under Bill Belichick, characterized by discipline, teamwork, adaptability, hard work, and a relentless pursuit of excellence. His approach prioritized the collective success of the team over individual achievements, demanding complete dedication from everyone involved. This led to unprecedented success, though it was also seen as rigid and demanding.

Belichick's coaching style is authoritative, meticulous, and intensely system-driven. His genius lies in unparalleled preparation, strategic acumen, and the ability to devise game plans that exploit opponent weaknesses. His emphasis was on discipline, precision, and the flawless execution of clearly defined roles. Every individual had a job, and the expectation was to do it perfectly. This created a highly efficient, disciplined machine where the team was greater than the sum of its parts.

A prime example is Super Bowl XXXVI, where the New England Patriots were significant underdogs against the high-powered St. Louis

Rams, known as "The Greatest Show on Turf" for their high-powered offense. The Patriots had already faced adversity, with young, relatively unknown Tom Brady stepping in for an injured starter. Belichick and his staff devised a brilliant and unconventional game plan, focusing on physicality to disrupt the Rams' receivers rather than trying to match their speed. This meticulous, tailored plan, based on exhaustive film study, showed his deep belief that intelligence and diligence could overcome raw talent, inspiring confidence in his players that they had a path to victory if they executed the plan. The team's roster wasn't filled with superstars; many key contributors were overlooked players. Belichick's system emphasized players understanding and flawlessly executing their roles. This highlighted that a well-coached team, where every player understands and executes their role, can compete with and defeat a team with more individual "stars." With the game tied at 17-17 and 1:30 left, Belichick famously chose to trust his young quarterback, Tom Brady, to lead a drive into field goal range, rather than playing conservatively for overtime. This composure and willingness to trust his players showcased his calculated aggression and belief in their preparation.

Belichick's feedback mechanism was primarily through clear expectations, constant evaluation, and accountability. The "Do Your Job" mantra itself was a continuous feedback loop—success was fulfilling your role, failure was not. This direct, performance-based feedback fostered immense accountability and a culture where players understood exactly what was expected.

Andy Reid: The Player-Centric Innovator

Now, consider the Kansas City Chiefs' culture under Andy Reid. Their culture is characterized by offensive innovation, a player-friendly environment, meticulous preparation, inclusivity, team unity, and trust in playmakers. It's a culture that balances the fun and creativity of Reid's offensive schemes with a strong work ethic and commitment to excellence.

When Andy Reid was hired by the Chiefs in January 2013, the franchise was at one of its lowest points, reeling from a dismal 2-14 record and a team tragedy. Reid immediately brought a sense of calm, stability, and proven leadership. His extensive experience provided instant credibility, and he implemented established processes emphasizing professionalism and accountability. This steady hand was foundational for a turnaround.

One of Reid's hallmark initiatives was establishing a "Player's Leadership Committee," where players, representing each position group, could voice concerns or suggestions directly to him. Crucially, Reid didn't just listen; he acted on reasonable concerns. This demonstrated genuine respect for the players and empowered them. It built trust rapidly because players saw their coach valued their input and was willing to adapt. Reid is renowned as a "teacher" of football, focusing on fundamentals and developing players. In his very first season (2013), the Chiefs, who had won only two games the previous year, went 11-5 and made the playoffs, a dramatic turnaround driven by his coaching and the cultural shift. His consistent demeanor through wins and losses built a resilient team that didn't panic under pressure.

Reid's coaching style is collaborative, player-centric, and adaptable. He's known as a brilliant offensive mind who also excels at connecting with his players on a personal level. His emphasis is on empowering players, fostering creativity (especially with talents like Mahomes), and building strong relationships. He adapts his system to maximize individual skills, unleashing player potential and transforming the Chiefs' organizational culture from struggling to thriving. His feedback mechanism relies on open communication and direct player involvement, exemplified by his "Player's Leadership Committee." His style is encouraging and collaborative, creating an environment where players feel safe enough to make mistakes, as long as they learn from them. This approach builds immense trust, which in turn fosters deep ownership and engagement.

Pat Summitt—The Unyielding Standard-Setter

Just as Bill Belichick and Andy Reid forged distinct paths to excellence in the NFL, the world of collegiate athletics offers another towering example of transformative coaching: Pat Summitt, the legendary head coach of the University of Tennessee Lady Volunteers basketball team. Summitt's career, spanning 38 years, was a masterclass in building a culture of relentless excellence, unwavering accountability, and profound personal development, culminating in 8 NCAA championships and an astounding 1,098 wins.

Summitt's coaching style was often described as "tough love." She was famously demanding, known for her intense "Summitt Stare" that could convey a myriad of messages without a single word. Her practices were rigorous, her expectations sky-high, and her feedback direct and unvarnished. Yet, beneath this demanding exterior lay a deep, unwavering commitment to her players as individuals, fostering a loyalty that propelled her teams to unprecedented heights.

The Culture of Accountability and Care

One of the most striking aspects of Summitt's culture was her absolute insistence on accountability, both on and off the court. She believed that every player had "potential greatness" within them, and her job was to push them to exceed what they thought they were capable of achieving. This wasn't merely about winning games; it was about preparing young women for success in life. A testament to this holistic approach is her remarkable **100 percent graduation rate** for every Lady Vol who completed her eligibility at Tennessee. This statistic, perhaps more than any championship, was her proudest achievement, demonstrating her commitment to their long-term well-being and growth beyond basketball.

Her philosophy was encapsulated in her "Definite Dozen" principles, which served as a blueprint for success in all aspects of life. Principles like "Take Full Responsibility," "Discipline Yourself So No One Else Has To," and "Make Hard Work Your Passion" were not just slogans; they were lived daily. Players knew that while Summitt pushed them to their limits, she also provided the support and care needed to reach them. As one former player famously quipped, "Yeah, I would recommend playing for Pat Summitt, if a year of counseling comes with it." This humorous statement highlights not only the intense challenge but also the undeniable growth and deep bond formed under her tutelage (CharacterandLeadership.com)

Building Trust Through Relentless Connection

Despite her reputation for sternness, Summitt's relationships with her players were deeply personal. She was known to visit players in the hospital during injuries, attend family funerals, and even host team meals at her home. These acts of genuine care, far removed from the basketball court, built a deep sense of trust and loyalty. Players understood that her demandingness stemmed from a place of love and a sincere belief in their potential. This demonstrated a critical aspect of effective feedback and coaching: "They don't care how much you know unless they know how much you care." Her consistent demonstration of care made her direct challenges acceptable and transformative.

Summitt also instilled a fierce competitive spirit. She lived by the mantra, "You can't always be the strongest or most talented or most gifted person in the room, but you can be the most competitive." This belief drove her to schedule challenging non-conference games and pushed her teams to constantly strive for improvement, even when they were at the top. She saw setbacks not as failures, but as opportunities to learn and grow, a true embodiment of a growth mindset.

The Ripple Effect in Action

Pat Summitt's impact extended far beyond her individual teams. She was a pioneer who helped legitimize women's basketball, attracting national attention and paving the way for future generations of female athletes and coaches. The "ripple effect" of her coaching is evident in the numerous former players who went on to become successful coaches themselves, carrying her demanding yet caring principles into their own programs. Her legacy underscores that coaching, at its most effective, is a human-centered endeavor where rigorous development and genuine connection combine to unlock extraordinary potential, both on and off the field.

From the Gridiron to the Sales Floor: A Business Coaching Case Study

Just as Bill Belichick, Andy Reid, and Pat Summitt forged distinct paths to excellence, these principles of culture-building and player-centric development are not confined to the athletic world. They come to life every day in the business world, often with the same dramatic impact. My experience working with a transformative sales leader at PowerSchool, a man I'll call "New Cool Craig," is a clear example of this ripple effect in a corporate setting.

When Craig arrived as the new Chief Revenue Officer, the sales organization was not consistently hitting its targets, and it lacked structure, unity, and a cohesive way to measure performance beyond the raw numbers. There was an opportunity to build a true team.

From day one, Craig demonstrated a coaching mindset. He and I partnered immediately to create a new framework for the sales organization. We built out metrics that went beyond targets and commissions; we focused on personal accountability, alignment with company culture, and emotional intelligence. This sent a clear message: How you sell is just as important as what you sell.

Craig's coaching style was a unique blend, much like the legends we've discussed. He was intensely competitive, once telling me, "If you and I are at a crosswalk, I am going to beat you to the other side." This drive for excellence was balanced with a deep authenticity and a commitment to his people. He restructured the team, not based on politics or tenure but by playing to each person's unique strengths.

I was able to witness his impact firsthand, as I joined his leadership team calls each morning, attended his staff meetings, and participated in the annual sales kick-off. In his meetings, he fostered an environment of psychological safety through humor and genuine connection. He would lead meetings while trying out different funny characters on Zoom or use unflattering screenshots of team members, you know when the screen freezes and the facial expression captured, as his virtual background, all in good fun. This lightheartedness built trust and made it safe for people to be themselves.

However, his standards were unyielding. He was famous for his mantra that he would not tolerate a "high-performing jerk." You could be a top performer, but you had to be a collaborative and respectful team member first. This was his version of Belichick's "Do Your Job" mantra, with a strong emphasis on character. He was direct with his feedback, but, because he had built such strong, authentic relationships, the feedback was received as a tool for growth not as a personal attack.

The result of Craig's coaching was transformative. He unified a disconnected team, soaring engagement *and* driving significant year-over-year growth. He proved that a leader can be demanding and empathetic, competitive and funny, data-driven and deeply human. He was a coach in the truest sense, and the ripples of his leadership strengthened the entire organization.

Coaches and Managers: Shared Responsibilities

The stories of Belichick, Reid, Summitt, and business leaders like Craig vividly illustrate the significant impact of coaching. Whether authoritative or collaborative, their styles differ, but their fundamental purpose is the same—and it overlaps significantly with that of a manager in any business setting.

At their core, both a sports coach and a manager share key responsibilities, focusing on individual development and performance as a means to collective success.

- **Skill Development:** A coach runs drills to improve a player's technique; a manager trains an employee on a new software. Both are responsible for developing the necessary skills on their team through ongoing feedback and guidance. Pat Summitt's "Definite Dozen" principles exemplify this, proving that great coaching develops not just professional skills but, crucially, life skills.
- **Performance Analysis and Improvement:** Coaches review game film and analyze player performance, identifying weaknesses, while managers monitor employee performance through metrics and reports. Both analyze data, pinpoint gaps, and develop strategies or plans to enhance performance. Summitt's immediate post-loss workouts and commitment to dissecting setbacks were her way of ensuring every performance served as a learning opportunity.
- **Strategy and Planning:** Coaches contribute to the overall game plan by developing position-specific strategies and adjusting tactics, similar to how managers contribute to the overall business plan by setting team goals and allocating resources. Both participate in planning and strategy sessions, aligning their specific focus area with broader objectives. Summitt's willingness to schedule

challenging opponents demonstrated her strategic vision for pushing her team's growth.

- **Player/Employee Evaluation:** Coaches evaluate player performance and identify potential for growth, just as managers evaluate employee performance through reviews and observations. Both assess individuals' capabilities, potential, and current performance to make decisions impacting team success and individual careers. Summitt's famous "Stare" was a direct, nonverbal evaluation tool, immediately communicating performance expectations and areas for improvement.
- **Mentorship and Motivation:** Coaches build relationships with players, provide encouragement, and offer guidance on personal and professional issues, mirroring how managers mentor employees, provide support, and foster a positive and productive work environment. Both play a role in developing and supporting individuals beyond their core tasks, inspiring them to reach their full potential. Pat Summitt excelled here, proving that her demandingness was rooted in care, as evidenced by her 100 percent graduation rate and her deep personal connections with every player.
- **Team Cohesion and Culture Building:** Both contribute to a positive team culture by fostering trust, communication, and mutual respect among players/employees and by addressing conflicts and promoting teamwork. They shape the team environment and try to create a space where people work well together. Summitt's insistence on accountability, loyalty, and her personal investments in her players forged an unbreakable team bond, making them a true family.

In essence, whether the goal is winning a Super Bowl, excellent patient care, or launching a new product, all roles are about developing people to achieve a common goal. The core principle is the same: Stronger, more capable individuals create stronger, more successful teams. This is the coaching mindset.

The Ripple from This Chapter

The first ripple from this chapter is a shift in your mindset. It's the decision to see your role not just as a manager of tasks but also as a coach of people. It's about believing, as Coach Zirzow and Pat Summitt did, that seeing potential is the first step to unlocking it. But let's be honest—belief alone doesn't pay the bills. In the corporate world, inspiration is wonderful, but results are required. This naturally leads to the most important question a skeptical CFO or a time-strapped manager could ask: "That's a great story, but does this coaching stuff actually work?" It's a fair question, and the answer is a resounding yes. In the next chapter, we're going to prove it.

Your Coaching Action Plan: Try This Today

The coaching mindset starts with a single choice: to see your role not just as a manager of tasks but as a coach of people. Here are five simple actions you can take today to begin creating your first ripple.

See the Unseen Potential. Think about one person on your team who might be overlooked. What is one talent or strength they have that you could help them see in themselves? Find a moment to name it and praise it.

Borrow a Coaching Style. Consider the coaching styles of Belichick, Reid, or Summitt. Which of their approaches resonates most with you? Which one is furthest from your natural style? Choose one small habit from a style you want to develop and try it out today.

Ask a "What/How" Question. The next time a team member comes to you with a problem, resist the urge to give them the answer. Instead, use a powerful question to guide them to their own solution. Try asking, "What have you explored so far?" or "How might we approach this?"

Find the Overlap. Look at your calendar for the coming week. Identify one task or meeting that is purely "management-focused" (e.g., a status update or a planning session). How can you reframe this to include a "coaching-focused" element? For example, during a status update, ask about a challenge they are facing.

Offer Partnership. End one of your daily conversations with a team member by offering partnership. Say, "I'm here to support you in navigating this. How can I best help?" This simple phrase transforms your role from a boss to a trusted partner.

CHAPTER 2

The Strategic Imperative— Quantifying the Ripple Effect on Business Growth

We've established the foundational mindset of coaching, that deep belief in human potential. But now we arrive at the ultimate bottom-line question: Does this "human-centered" stuff actually work? It's a fair question! While good intentions are lovely, results pay the bills. In this chapter, we move from the philosophical to the financial. We will unveil how a coaching culture doesn't just change lives; it reshapes an organization's financial landscape, turning potential into pure profit.

The numbers might surprise you. The research paints a clear picture: Investing in a coaching approach unlocks staggering financial returns, boosts productivity, and builds a more resilient and engaged workforce. The power of great coaching is not anecdotal; it is substantiated by compelling data. So, let's explore the powerful business case for making coaching a cornerstone of your leadership.

Quantifying the Impact: The Tangible Returns of Coaching

The financial case for coaching isn't just strong; it's practically a cheat code for business success. Study after study demonstrates it as a sound investment that directly contributes to the bottom line. While most investments are happy with a single-digit return, coaching operates on a different planet. Consider the returns: A global survey by PriceWaterhouseCoopers reported an average ROI of seven times the initial investment in coaching. The International Society for Performance Improvement found that coaching yields a 221 percent ROI. And when a MetrixGlobal study included the financial gains from higher productivity and retention, the ROI for executive coaching soared to an incredible 788 percent. You'd have to invent a time machine and buy Apple stock in 1999 to get a return like that. Where else can you possibly get this kind of return?

Where else can you possibly get this kind of return? Here's some interesting data.

The International Coaching Federation (ICF) reports the following statistics on the benefits of executive coaching:

- **70** percent **increase** in individual performance
- **50** percent **increase** in team performance
- **48** percent **increase** in organizational performance

Organizations that offer training alone experience a **22** percent increase in productivity, but, when combined with coaching, that figure rises to **88** percent (Olivero et al. 1999; Matuson 2023).

Increased Productivity: Coaching can boost productivity by as much as **44** percent, as demonstrated by a *Harvard Business Review* study. When combined with training, coaching can increase productivity by an average of **86** percent.

- **Improved Work Performance:** Coaching can help employees develop new skills, understand job requirements, and take ownership of their responsibilities, leading to better work performance.
- **Enhanced Self-Confidence and Well-being:** Coaching can significantly boost self-confidence, improve relationships, and enhance effective communication skills.
- **Increased Engagement and Motivation:** By focusing on personal and professional development, coaching can create a more engaged and motivated workforce.
- **Reduced Turnover:** Coaching can lead to a more engaged and motivated workforce, which can reduce employee turnover.

The consistent reporting of high ROI figures across multiple reputable sources indicates that the benefits of coaching are not simply additive but often multiplicative. For example, improved leadership, a common outcome of coaching, can lead to higher employee engagement, which in turn reduces turnover and boosts overall productivity—each contributing significantly to financial gains. The **788** percent figure, specifically highlighting the inclusion of retention benefits, underscores how addressing one area, such as leadership effectiveness, can trigger a cascade of financial benefits by mitigating significant organizational costs. This suggests that organizations should view coaching not merely as an expense but as a strategic capital investment in human potential that generates compounding financial returns through improved efficiency, reduced costs, and enhanced revenue generation.

Concrete examples further illustrate these significant financial gains. Intel's internal coaching program, for instance, now contributes approximately US$1 billion per year in operating margin, demonstrating a profound transformation across all business units. Intel recognizes the importance of investing in its employees and their technical expertise in order to achieve the best outcomes. Results were a 2.7 times higher promotion rate among leaders, a 91 percent score for whether coaches achieved business goals, and 91 percent of participants indicating that they gained tools and techniques to elevate their leadership skills.

Organizations that cultivate a strong coaching culture also report remarkable financial performance, with +27 percent year-over-year revenue growth and achieving +87 percent net profit margins. Additionally, these organizations report 47 percent higher revenue per employee compared to those without strong coaching cultures.

The exceptional financial impact observed in the Intel example and the statistics tied to "strong coaching cultures" reveal a critical distinction: While individual coaching yields high ROI, the magnitude of financial impact scales dramatically when coaching principles are embedded throughout the entire organization. This indicates that a systemic approach to coaching fosters behaviors and efficiencies that drive enterprise-level financial performance, extending beyond isolated improvements. For businesses aiming for transformative financial outcomes, the objective should therefore extend beyond offering coaching to select individuals; it should encompass cultivating a pervasive coaching culture that fundamentally reshapes how work is done, leading to sustained and significant boosts in revenue and profitability.

From the HR Deck: Turning New Leaders into Navigators
One of the leakiest buckets in any company's budget is the "new leader ramp-up time." A new Director or VP is a massive investment, but for the first six months, they're often just trying to figure out who's who, how to get a budget approved, and the secret art of "how to get things done around here without stepping on a political landmine." From my seat in HR, I could see the hidden costs of this slow ramp-up in delayed projects and team uncertainty.

We knew we could do better than just handing them a laptop and a link to the org chart.

So, I worked with my Learning & Development Manager to establish a leadership cohort program for our new Directors and above. The idea was simple but powerful: we created small groups that paired our newest leaders with two or three Directors who were already one or two years into their roles. These weren't grizzled veterans; they were leaders who had just successfully navigated the challenges the new leaders were facing. They became a sort of group mentor, or a team of navigators.

This wasn't a fluffy meet-and-greet. It was a structured, six-month program. We covered the non-negotiable essentials—understanding the company P&L, budgeting, and finance. But the real magic was in the unscripted parts. The rest of the agenda was left to the group to decide what was most needed. This created a space for them to have real, honest conversations about the challenges they were facing.

When it came time to justify the investment for this program, we didn't frame it as "leadership training." We framed it as a strategic business initiative. By creating this peer-coaching ecosystem, we were directly addressing key business metrics:

We were accelerating the time-to-impact for our most critical talent. Getting a new Director fully effective in four months instead of eight has a massive, positive financial ripple.

We were increasing the retention of our senior leaders. A new leader who feels supported and connected from day one is far less likely to leave.

We were building a self-sustaining coaching culture. The program had a brilliant secondary effect: it signaled to our more tenured Directors that part of their role was to develop the next wave of leaders.

This is the perfect example of how a "soft skill" like coaching, when applied systemically, becomes a hard-nosed business strategy.

Productivity and Performance Gains: Optimizing Human Output

Beyond financial returns, coaching directly enhances individual and team performance, leading to measurable improvements in output and efficiency. Over **70** percent of individuals who receive coaching report benefits from improved work performance, relationships, and communication. A particularly compelling finding highlights the synergy between training and coaching: When training is paired with coaching, individuals boost their productivity by an average of **86** percent, a stark contrast to the mere **22** percent increase observed from training alone. This significant difference suggests that traditional training, while imparting knowledge, often falls short in translating that knowledge into sustained behavioral change and measurable productivity gains. Coaching provides the crucial personalized application, reinforcement, accountability, and feedback loop necessary to solidify learning and ensure its practical implementation. Consequently, organizations should integrate coaching as a fundamental component of their learning and development strategies to maximize the ROI of all training investments, ensuring that skills acquired translate directly into enhanced productivity and goal attainment.

Coaching clients are also significantly more likely to achieve their goals compared to those who do not utilize coaching. Furthermore, coaching improves critical cognitive and strategic capabilities. A *Harvard Business Review* study found that **71** percent of executives who received coaching improved their decision-making abilities. Companies that foster a strong coaching culture also demonstrate a **14** percent **boost** in problem-solving capabilities and a **21** percent **increase** in team innovation compared to their counterparts.

In today's volatile and complex business environment, the capacity to make rapid, informed decisions, creatively solve unforeseen problems, and continuously innovate is paramount for organizational survival and growth. Coaching provides leaders with objective perspectives and frameworks to sharpen these essential skills, fostering a proactive and adaptive mindset. Thus, investing in coaching is a direct investment in an organization's intellectual capital and its capacity for strategic agility, enabling it to navigate uncertainty, seize new opportunities, and maintain a leading edge in the market.

The Hidden Costs of Churn: Why Investing in People Pays Off

While we've explored the immense returns of a coaching culture, it's equally vital to understand the often-underestimated costs of not cultivating one. There's a persistent, sometimes even celebrated, mindset in some organizations that a certain percentage of employee churn (e.g., 10 percent) is a healthy goal. The idea, of course, is that it "cleans out" underperformers or brings in "fresh blood." This is like saying a small, persistent leak in your boat is a healthy way to get rid of old water. But let's be honest: While not every employee is the right fit for every role or team, and some departures are indeed necessary, a high churn rate is rarely a sign of health. More often, it's a symptom of a deeper issue, and its costs far outweigh any perceived benefits.

Consider the true price of an employee exit, even a seemingly "managed" one:

- **Direct Financial Costs:** This is the obvious part, but it's staggering. It includes:
  - **Recruitment:** Advertising, agency fees, recruiter salaries, and background checks
  - **Onboarding:** HR time, IT setup, initial training materials, and manager's time
  - **Training and Development:** The investment in skills and knowledge that walks out the door
  - Severance and Benefits Continuation: If applicable
  - Estimates vary, but replacing a single employee can cost anywhere from 50 percent to 200 percent of their annual salary, depending on the role's seniority and specialization.

- **Indirect, Yet Significant, Costs (The Invisible Ripple of Damage):** These are harder to quantify but hit the bottom line just as hard, if not harder:
    - **Lost Productivity:** The time between an employee leaving and their replacement becoming fully productive. Projects stall, deadlines are missed, and the remaining team often has to shoulder extra work.
    - **Morale Erosion:** When colleagues see valued team members leave, or when there's a constant revolving door, it sends a clear message: "The company doesn't care." And when people feel the company doesn't care, they start to not care. This disengagement is a silent killer of innovation and effort.
    - **Knowledge Drain:** Critical institutional knowledge, client relationships, and process expertise walk out the door, forcing the organization to rebuild from scratch.
    - **Customer Service Issues:** New employees take time to get up to speed, potentially leading to slower response times, inconsistent service, or a dip in client satisfaction.
    - **Project Delays and Quality Dips:** Inexperienced teams or stretched resources can lead to project setbacks, rework, and a decline in the quality of deliverables.
    - **Damaged Employer Brand:** A reputation for high turnover makes it harder and more expensive to attract top talent in the future.

This isn't just about losing a body; it's about losing momentum, trust, and the very fabric of your team's cohesion. The "10 percent churn is healthy" mantra often overlooks the fact that many of those departures could have been prevented with proactive, human-centered leadership.

How Coaching Acts as a Preventative Measure:

This is precisely where a coaching culture becomes your most powerful defense against costly churn. By consistently providing feedback, support, and opportunities for growth, you:

- **Identify Misalignments Early:** Regular coaching conversations allow leaders to spot emerging issues with skills, motivation, or cultural fit *before* they become critical.

- **Bridge Skill Gaps:** Instead of letting an employee flounder, coaching provides targeted development, turning potential underperformers into valuable contributors.
- **Boost Engagement and Belonging:** When employees feel seen, heard, and invested in, their loyalty naturally increases. They become part of the team's success story.
- **Foster a Growth Mindset:** Feedback becomes a tool for development and not a precursor to dismissal. This makes employees more resilient and adaptable.

In essence, while the "When the Ripple Hits a Wall" section acknowledges that some departures are inevitable, this section emphasizes that many are *not*. They are the direct result of a lack of proactive investment in people. A coaching culture isn't just about attracting and developing talent; it's about *retaining* it, transforming potential exits into powerful examples of growth and commitment.

Research on the Impact of Frequent Coaching Feedback on the Bottom Line

Research shows coaching programs providing regular, ongoing feedback significantly outpace traditional annual reviews for ROI. Companies investing in coaching see measurable improvements: **70** percent **increase** in individual performance and up to **50** percent team performance; **86** percent of companies reported recouping investment, with ROI as high as **10 to 49 times** initial spend. Regular coaching provides immediate, actionable feedback for real-time behavior adjustment, unlike waiting for an annual audit.

Organizations replacing or supplementing annual reviews with frequent coaching see significant benefits in engagement and retention, factors tied to the bottom line. Cleveland Clinic's coaching program contributed around **$85 million** in physician retention. The International Trade Administration achieved **225** percent **ROI** by boosting productivity and strengthening alignment. Ongoing dialogue makes employees feel seen/supported, reducing turnover and costly disruptions.

Frequent coaching impacts overall business performance. Reviews report organizations with strong coaching cultures reported higher revenue

(**51** percent), better decision making, faster problem resolution, and healthier team dynamics. By creating regular feedback/accountability, organizations report improved innovation, agility, and a stronger culture. Personalized coaching embeds coaching behaviors across the organization, multiplying impact.

The Ripple from This Chapter: The ripple from this chapter is one of conviction. The data is clear: Investing in coaching isn't an expense; it's an investment with one of the highest returns available in business. We've seen the staggering ROI, the boosts in productivity, and the powerful defense it provides against costly turnover. So now, the question is no longer "Is it worth it?" The question becomes, "Am I ready to do it?" The numbers prove the *what* and the *why*, making it clear that coaching isn't a "soft skill"—it's a financial powerhouse. But a beautiful theory is only as good as the tools you have to put it into practice. The next chapter is all about the *how*: your manager's playbook for getting it done.

Your Coaching Action Plan: Try This Today

You've seen the data that prove coaching is a powerful business strategy. Now, here are five actions you can take today to start turning that theory into practice.

- **Calculate the Cost of Churn.** Think about one recent team member departure. Take 15 minutes to list out the time and money spent on recruitment, onboarding, and lost productivity. Put a rough dollar amount on it. This makes the hidden cost of a disengaged culture tangible.
- **Track a "Soft" Metric.** Choose a new hire on your team. Over the next month, track their "time to full productivity"—when they started versus when they were fully functional. Use this as a baseline to demonstrate how your coaching can accelerate ramp-up time for future hires.
- **Link a "Soft Skill" to a "Hard" Goal.** In your next one-on-one, ask a team member: "What's one goal you want to achieve this quarter, and what's one skill we can develop together to help you get there?" This explicitly ties their personal growth to a business outcome.

- **Run an ROI Check-in.** The next time a team member brings up a challenge or a project delay, frame your coaching around return on investment. Ask, "What's the cost of not solving this right now?" and "What's the potential upside if we find a solution?"
- **Frame the Investment.** Think about one piece of professional development you want for a team member (e.g., a conference, a new certification, or a training program). Instead of framing it as an expense, write a one-paragraph summary to your manager explaining the potential return on investment for the team, the project, or the company.

CHAPTER 3

Developing Your Coaching Skills—A Path for Every Manager

So, we've established that coaching isn't just a fluffy concept; it's a financial powerhouse. The data are compelling, and the business case is clear. Now, the natural (and perhaps slightly daunting) question arises: "Okay, I'm sold. But how do I actually *do* this?"

Well, the good news is, you don't need to be a sports legend or have a degree in psychology. So, in this chapter, we're going to dive into the must-have (and totally learnable!) skills that help people spark real change—using good old-fashioned purposeful, effective communication. Think of it as your roadmap for inspiring others, minus the awkward small talk and with a dash of friendly wit.

From the HR Deck: The Myth of the "Natural" Coach
Every year, during talent reviews, I hear managers say, "I'm just not a natural coach." They see coaching as an innate personality trait not a learnable skill. From an HR perspective, this is one of the biggest barriers to building a true coaching culture. My role isn't just to provide training; it's to reframe the entire concept. We've had success by integrating coaching competencies directly into our performance management system. When "asking powerful questions" or "giving SBI feedback" becomes a measurable part of a manager's review, it shifts from a "nice-to-have" personality trait to a "must-have" professional skill. We build the cultural infrastructure to support the skill, proving it can be developed by anyone.

For some, coaching might feel like a natural extension of their personality—perhaps they're inherently empathetic listeners or naturally inclined to ask probing questions (for those who have taken the DiSC assessment, I identify as a Coach—SIc). But what if that's not you? What if the idea of guiding someone to find their own solutions feels less intuitive than simply telling them what to do?

Coaching is not just an innate talent; it's a set of learnable skills and a conscious approach that can be cultivated with effort and practice. Management today requires more than just giving instructions. It demands the ability to help people grow, bring out their best, and empower them. This is where coaching comes in, focusing on seeing potential and helping others discover it. Even if this doesn't come naturally, you can absolutely develop these capabilities.

Understanding Your Starting Point: Self-Awareness as a Foundation

Becoming an effective coach begins with deep self-awareness. You need to understand your own preferred approach, core values, natural communication style, and personality traits. This isn't about changing who you are—it is about understanding your natural tendencies and how they can be leveraged or might need adjustment for effective coaching. This foundation will help you develop an authentic coaching style that feels true to you, making it more sustainable and impactful.

You can explore your current style and identify areas for growth through several avenues:

- **Self-Reflection and Journaling:** Dedicate time to think about your past experiences.
  - ○ **Prompts:** Who were your most impactful mentors or leaders (like my Coach Zirzow)? What specific actions did they take that resonated with you? When have you felt most effective in helping someone else learn or grow? What were the circumstances? What are your core values (e.g., integrity, collaboration, innovation, efficiency, empathy)? How do these values

currently show up in your interactions, and how could they guide your coaching?

- ○ **Action:** Keep a coaching journal. After a conversation where you tried to coach, write down what went well, what felt awkward, and what you might try differently next time.
- Formal Assessments and Feedback:
  - ○ **Personality Assessments:** Tools like DiSC, CliftonStrengths, or Myers-Briggs can provide insights into your natural preferences for communication, decision making, and interaction. Understanding your own profile can help you anticipate how you might naturally approach coaching and where you might need to stretch.
  - ○ **360-Degree Feedback:** Crucially, seek feedback from others—your direct reports, peers, and your own manager—on your current leadership and communication style. Ask specific questions like, "When have you felt most supported by me?" or "What's one thing I could do differently to help you grow more?" This provides an external perspective on how your current interactions are perceived.
- **Observe and Learn:** Pay attention to how other effective coaches operate. What specific phrases do they use? How do they structure conversations? What's their demeanor? You don't need to copy them, but you can identify techniques that resonate with your authentic self.

Aligning Your Values and Personality with Coaching: Once you have a clearer picture, you can work on aligning your approach with core coaching values. For example, if you deeply value **integrity**, your coaching should always be honest and transparent. If **collaboration** is key, your coaching will naturally involve more co-creation of solutions. You can leverage your existing personality strengths—perhaps you're analytical and can help structure problem-solving, or maybe you're great at building rapport, which is key for empathy. Identifying weaknesses allows you to focus your learning and practice where it's most needed, ensuring that your coaching feels authentic and powerful.

Mastering the Learnable Skills of Coaching

The foundation of effective coaching lies in several key, learnable skills. These are not reserved for those with a specific "coaching personality"; they are techniques that can be learned and honed through conscious practice.

Active Listening: The Art of Truly Hearing
- **What It Is:** This is fundamental. It's not just hearing words but truly understanding someone's message, meaning, and emotions—both what's said and what's unsaid. It's about being fully present and nonjudgmental.
- How to practice:
  - Maintain Eye Contact and Open Body Language: Show you're engaged. Avoid crossing your arms or looking at your phone.
  - Resist Interruption: Let the other person finish their thoughts completely. Practice comfortable silence.
  - Use Verbal Cues: "Mm-hmm," "I see," "Go on…"
  - Paraphrase/Summarize: "So, if I understand correctly, you're feeling frustrated because…?" or "It sounds like the main challenge is X." This confirms understanding and makes the other person feel heard.
  - Ask Clarifying Questions: "Could you tell me more about that?" or "What exactly do you mean by 'overwhelmed'?"
  - Pay Attention to Nonverbal Cues: Tone of voice, facial expressions, and gestures often tell a deeper story.

Example: Instead of jumping in with a solution when an employee says, "I'm really struggling with this new software," an active listener might respond, "It sounds like this software is causing some significant frustration. Can you tell me more about what specifically is proving difficult?"

Powerful Questioning: Guiding Discovery, Not Giving Answers

- **What It Is:** This skill shifts the focus from you giving answers to helping others find their own. It involves asking open-ended questions that stimulate reflection, self-discovery, and new insights. The goal is to empower, not to interrogate.

- How to Practice:
  - Focus on "What" and "How": These questions encourage deeper thought. Avoid "why" questions, which can sound accusatory.
  - Problem-Solving: "What have you explored so far?" "How might you approach this differently?" "What's the ideal outcome you're hoping for?"
  - Goal-Setting: "What does success look like for you in this role?" "How will you know you've achieved it?" "What's the first step you can take?"
  - Development: "What skills do you want to strengthen?" "How do you envision yourself growing in the next year?" "What support do you need from me?"
  - Be Comfortable with Silence: After asking a powerful question, resist the urge to fill the silence. Give the other person time to think and formulate their own answer.
    - Follow-Up Questions: Build on their responses. "And what else?" "What makes you say that?" "What's the biggest challenge in that idea?"

Example: When an employee says, "I don't know how to solve this problem," instead of "You should try X," a powerful questioner might ask, "Given what you know about the situation, what are two or three potential paths you could explore, even if they seem unconventional?"

Operationalizing Empathy: From Feeling to Action

We all know what empathy feels like, but how do you actually *do* it when your inbox is overflowing and a deadline is looming? It's not about becoming a therapist; it's about micro-moments of genuine connection that build trust and make your team feel truly seen. For an INFJ, this might come naturally but translating that deep understanding into actionable leadership behaviors is the key.

Here are concrete ways to operationalize empathy in your daily leadership:

- **Practice Active Presence:** Put away distractions during 1:1s or team discussions. Give your full attention. This simple act communicates respect and care more than words ever could.
- **Acknowledge Emotions First:** Before jumping to solutions, validate their feelings. "It sounds like you're feeling frustrated with this process" or "I can see why that would be a challenging situation." This doesn't mean agreeing with their perspective, but acknowledging their emotional experience creates a safe space.
- **Remember the Small Details:** Recall a personal detail they shared (e.g., "How was your daughter's soccer game?"). These small acts show you listen and care beyond their work output.
- **Offer "Space to Vent":** Sometimes, people just need to be heard. Resist the urge to immediately fix, advise, or problem-solve. Simply listen, nod, and offer supportive cues. "Tell me more about that" or "What's on your mind?"
- **Ask Empathetic Questions:** Instead of "Why didn't you do X?" try "What challenges did you face with X?" or "What support do you need to move forward?" This shifts from judgment to understanding.
- **Show Vulnerability (Appropriately):** Sharing a brief, relatable struggle of your own (where you learned something) can foster connection and show you're human too, building reciprocal empathy.
- **"Check-in" Beyond Tasks:** Occasionally, a quick chat message or a brief verbal check-in that has nothing to do with a task, but simply asks about their well-being, can make a huge difference. "How are things going for you this week, generally?"

These micro-moments, consistently applied, transform empathy from a feeling into a powerful leadership practice that builds trust, strengthens relationships, and creates a foundation for all other coaching efforts to thrive.

The Art of Difficult Conversations:
Beyond Performance Feedback

Let's be honest, few things make a leader want to suddenly "remember" an urgent dental appointment more than the prospect of mediating a team conflict or addressing a colleague's less-than-stellar behavior. We've all been there, mentally rehearsing the conversation a hundred times, only to stumble over the first sentence. Your carefully crafted, empathetic monologue suddenly comes out sounding like a GPS navigator recalculating in a tunnel. But just like a coach strategizes for game day, you can approach these talks with clarity and courage, transforming potential landmines into opportunities for growth and stronger team cohesion.

While providing constructive performance feedback is crucial, leaders often face other types of difficult conversations that require a similar, human-centered, coaching approach. These aren't about skill gaps, but about behavioral issues, conflict, or delivering tough news.

Here's how to approach these dreaded dialogues with a coaching mindset:

- Mediating Team Conflict:
  - **Challenge:** Two team members are clashing, impacting team harmony.
  - **Coaching Approach:** Instead of dictating a solution, facilitate a dialogue. Meet with each individual separately first to understand their perspective (active listening, empathy). Then, bring them together, setting clear ground rules for respectful communication. Focus on shared goals and the impact of the conflict on the team. Ask, "What outcome are we both aiming for here?" and "What's one step you can each take to improve this dynamic?"
- Addressing Behavioral Issues (Nonperformance):
  - **Challenge:** A team member is consistently late or exhibits unprofessional conduct (e.g., gossiping, negativity).
  - **Coaching Approach:** Use the SBI model (Situation–Behavior–Impact) to keep it objective and focused on observable actions, not on character. "In yesterday's meeting, when you

interrupted Sarah multiple times (Behavior), it made others hesitate to share ideas (Impact) and slowed down our decision making (Impact)." Then, pivot to coaching: "What do you think is contributing to this, and what approach could you try next time?" Frame it as aligning with team values and professional growth.

- Delivering Bad News (e.g., Project Cancellation, Budget Cuts):
  - **Challenge:** Communicating decisions that will negatively impact your team.
  - **Coaching Approach:** Be transparent and empathetic, but firm on the facts. Acknowledge the emotional impact ("I know this is disappointing news…"). Explain the *why* behind the decision clearly. Then, shift to what *is* within their control and how you will support them. "While this project is ending, what opportunities do you see for applying your skills elsewhere?" or "How can I best support you through this transition?"
- Saying "No" Effectively:
  - **Challenge:** A team member comes with a request you can't approve (e.g., a new project, a resource request).
  - **Coaching Approach:** Don't just say "no." Explain the *reason* behind the "no" (e.g., context, priorities, or resources). Offer alternatives or coach them to find solutions that *do* align. "I understand why that project is exciting, but given our current strategic priorities, we need to focus our resources on X. What's another way you could achieve a similar impact within our current focus?"

These conversations are never easy, but by applying your coaching skills—active listening, powerful questioning, empathy, and constructive, impact-focused feedback—you can navigate them with integrity, preserve relationships, and even foster growth in the face of adversity. It's about leading with courage, even when the conversation feels anything but comfortable.

Patience and Persistence: The Long Game of Growth
What It Is: Recognize that growth and change take time. Coaching is not a one-off event; it's an ongoing process. As a coach, you need to provide consistent support, encouragement, and understanding, helping people learn from setbacks and celebrating incremental progress.

How to Practice:
- **Manage Expectations**: Understand that behavioral change is slow. Don't expect immediate transformations.
- **Celebrate Small Wins:** Acknowledge effort, learning, and small improvements, not just big breakthroughs.
- **Be a Consistent Presence:** Regular check-ins, even brief ones, reinforce your commitment to their development.
- **Learn from Setbacks:** When things don't go as planned, frame it as a learning opportunity. "What did we learn from this?" "How can we apply that next time?"

Example: An employee tries a new approach based on your coaching, and it doesn't work perfectly. Instead of "That didn't quite hit the mark," try: "I appreciate you taking that risk and trying something new. What insights did you gain from this attempt, and what might you adjust for next time?"

Best Practices for Coaching

- **Establish Clear Goals and Structure** using frameworks like the GROW (Goal, Reality, Options, Will) model.
- Foster a Trust-Based Relationship built on psychological safety.
- **Use Active Listening and Tailored Feedback**, employing specific, constructive feedback, reflective listening, and open-ended questioning.
- **Encourage Self-Reflection and Accountability** through journaling or self-assessments.
- Adapt to Individual Learning Styles (visual, hands-on, verbal).
- **Maintain Consistency and Follow-Up** through regular check-ins. Ongoing coaching leads to sustained behavioral change.

Putting Skills into Practice: The Iterative Cycle of Coaching

Even with foundational skills, effective coaching is not a one-size-fits-all approach. Learning to adapt your style based on individual needs, personalities, and career stages (often called situational coaching) is a crucial skill to develop. The examples of coaches like Steve Kerr adjusting his approach and Gregg Popovich tailoring his guidance for Tony Parker illustrate the importance of flexibility.

Developing your coaching skills is an iterative process, much like refining a new stroke in swimming. It requires consistent practice, reflection, and a willingness to continuously learn and adapt.

- **Practice Deliberately:** Look for daily opportunities to apply these skills—in 1:1s, team meetings, informal chats. The more you practice, the more natural these behaviors will become.
- **Seek Feedback on Your Coaching:** Just as you give feedback, actively ask your team members for feedback on your coaching style. "What could I do differently to be a more effective coach for you?" This models vulnerability and shows your commitment to growth.
- **Reflect and Adjust:** After a coaching conversation, take a few minutes to reflect. What went well? What could have been better? How did the other person respond? Use these insights to refine your approach for the next interaction.
- **Be Patient with Yourself:** You won't be a perfect coach overnight. Embrace a growth mindset for your own development as well. Celebrate your progress and learn from your missteps.

Learning to coach effectively, even when it feels unnatural initially, is a journey that involves consistent practice and persistence. By consciously focusing on these learnable aspects—active listening, powerful questioning, empathy, constructive feedback, empowerment, and patience—you can build your capacity to lead and develop others, creating that powerful ripple effect of growth discussed throughout these pages. Providing training on how to give and receive feedback is also a critical step organization can take to equip everyone with these skills.

Leading Researchers on Coaching Feedback

- **Daniel Kluger and Angelo DeNisi**: Feedback Intervention Theory (FIT). Their foundational work established FIT, which posits that feedback is effective when it directs attention toward a comparison between current behavior and a desired standard or goal. A key insight from FIT is that feedback's impact isn't universal; its effectiveness hinges on how it's perceived and interpreted by the recipient and what level of self-regulation it activates. They emphasize that feedback is most potent when it focuses on task-level information, helping individuals understand how to bridge the gap between their current performance and their goals, rather than merely highlighting the discrepancy.

- **Richard Boyatzis**: Resonant Leadership and Positive Emotional Attractors. A prominent researcher in emotional intelligence and leadership development, Boyatzis emphasizes the importance of resonant leadership and its connection to coaching. He argues that effective coaching transcends merely addressing deficits; it focuses on nurturing strengths, sparking vision, and fostering a positive emotional attractor. His work highlights that feedback should be delivered in a way that builds empathy and inspires individuals toward their ideal self rather than simply pointing out areas for improvement. This "coaching with compassion" approach is crucial for sustainable insight and growth, creating a powerful wave of positive emotion and engagement.

- **Qing Wang, Yi-Ling Lai, Xiaobo Xu, and Almuth McDowall**: Empirical Evidence of Coaching Effectiveness. These researchers have contributed significant empirical evidence on the effectiveness of workplace coaching. Through rigorous meta-analyses, they have statistically demonstrated that coaching interventions reliably enhance various outcomes, particularly goal attainment and self-efficacy. Their work provides strong, data-driven support for the tangible benefits of coaching, showing that it consistently helps individuals set and achieve goals, and significantly boosts their belief in their own capabilities—a critical component for sustained performance and the surge of positive emotion and engagement.

- **Dr. Andriana Eliadis: Neuroscience of Feedback.** Dr. Eliadis's research delves into the neuroscience of feedback, exploring how timely and balanced feedback triggers beneficial neural processes within the brain. Her work suggests that feedback, when delivered optimally, can activate brain regions associated with learning, reward, and self-awareness, making the recipient more receptive to information and more motivated to change. This underscores the extreme importance of the how and when of feedback delivery, aligning with the idea that well-timed, constructive input can literally rewire neural pathways for accelerated growth and a more impactful ripple.

- **Carolyn Wilson, Jennifer Zamora, and Guangrong Dai (Korn Ferry Institute)**: Translating Research into Actionable Strategies. These researchers, often working from a practical, applied perspective within a leadership development context, focus on translating academic insights into actionable strategies for organizations. Their work typically involves identifying the specific leadership behaviors that drive talent development and performance and then creating frameworks, tools, and training programs that enable leaders to apply coaching principles effectively in their daily roles. They bridge the gap between theoretical research and practical implementation, providing clear guidance on how to build strong coaching cultures that create measurable ripples of success.

In essence, these researchers collectively underscore that effective coaching feedback is not just about what you say, but *how, when, and why* you say it, always with an eye toward fostering genuine growth, trust, and self-efficacy in the recipient.

The Ripple from This Chapter: The ripple from this chapter is one of capability. You now have the core tools of a great coach in your toolkit: active listening, powerful questioning, and a framework for giving feedback that builds people up. But having a hammer doesn't make you a master carpenter. The art of coaching isn't just knowing the skills; it's knowing precisely how and when to use them. How do you adapt your approach for the go-getter who craves challenge versus the rising talent who needs confidence?

Your Coaching Action Plan: Try This Today

- **Reflect and Discover Your Style:** Take 10 minutes to journal about a time you felt most effective in helping someone grow. What did you do? What core values were present?
- **Practice Active Listening:** In your next 1:1 or team meeting, challenge yourself to only listen and ask clarifying questions for the first 5 minutes. Resist giving advice.
- **Ask a "What/How" Question:** Instead of offering a solution to a colleague's problem, ask, "What are some ways you've considered approaching this?" or "How might you take the first step?"
- **Deliver SBI Feedback:** Identify one recent situation where you can give specific, behavior-based feedback (positive or constructive) using the Situation–Behavior–Impact model.
- **Offer Partnership:** Find an opportunity today to tell a team member, "I'm here to support you in navigating this. How can I best help?"

CHAPTER 4

Situational Coaching— Adapting Your Style for Maximum Impact

We've spent the last chapter sharpening our coaching tools. But a tool is only as effective as the person wielding it. Just as Coach Zirzow didn't coach every swimmer the same way, impactful leadership requires a nuanced touch. Now that we have the core skills, we'll explore the art of situational coaching—how to fine-tune your approach to unlock the best in each person, rather than expecting everyone to fit a single mold.

Effective coaching isn't a one-size-fits-all approach. Just as a coach tailors a training regimen for a star athlete versus a new recruit, you must adapt your style to each team member's individual needs, personalities, and career stage. This is known as situational coaching. I experienced this firsthand when former team members joined me in a new VP role. Even though I knew them, they were at vastly different career points and required distinct coaching. Though familiar, they were at vastly different career points and required distinct coaching.

It became evident that truly impactful coaching required a shift in perspective. Instead of simply directing tasks and evaluating outcomes, I prioritized understanding each employee on a deeper level. This involved taking the time to engage in meaningful conversations, actively listening to their perspectives, and inquiring about their career goals and personal motivations. By fostering these strong interpersonal relationships, I created a foundation of trust and open communication, which proved essential for effective coaching.

Discovering what truly motivated each individual was a critical aspect of this personalized approach. For some, it might have been the opportunity for professional development and skill enhancement. For others, it could have been the desire for increased autonomy and responsibility, or perhaps the recognition and appreciation for their contributions. By understanding these intrinsic drivers, I could tailor my coaching strategies to align with their individual needs and aspirations, fostering a greater sense of engagement and ownership.

Furthermore, I recognized the importance of adapting my coaching style to suit each employee's learning preferences and communication style. Some individuals responded well to direct and concise feedback, while others thrived in a more collaborative and supportive environment. Some preferred structured guidance and clear expectations, while others benefited from more open-ended exploration and creative problem-solving. By being flexible and adaptable in my approach, I could ensure that my coaching was received effectively and had the greatest positive impact on their growth and development.

Let's look at a few examples from my own experience:

Case Study 1: Empowering the Go-Getter

How Coaching Ignited a Career Path—My Go-Getter HR Business Partner was driven, smart, positive, and personable—a valuable asset who consistently exceeded expectations in her role. She thrived in an environment where her contributions were acknowledged and celebrated, demonstrating a strong desire for recognition. Clear and well-defined goals provided her with the necessary direction and motivation to excel, and she greatly valued understanding her potential career trajectory within the company.

My coaching approach centered on collaboratively establishing ambitious yet attainable targets that would challenge her and foster professional growth. We dedicated time to strategically planning her long-term career aspirations, identifying potential opportunities and necessary steps for advancement. Recognizing her inherent drive and capabilities, my role as a coach was primarily to provide a supportive framework, offer challenging assignments, and create dedicated space for her to independently develop and execute her own plans, offering guidance and insights when needed, while empowering her to take ownership of her professional journey. This approach allowed her to leverage her strengths and develop crucial leadership skills, ultimately creating a positive effect within her team and the wider organization.

Some of the specific support I provided her was to prepare her to move into a leadership role. We collaborated on what that could look like as far as opportunities that I could provide that would give her opportunities to lead, such as projects and team meetings. She recently confirmed that she is now in a management role at her current company.

Case Study 2: From Overwhelm to Empowerment: Coaching a Dedicated Leader

The Dedicated Total Rewards Manager was a highly valued member of the organization, known for his unwavering commitment to his team's well-being and professional development. He possessed a strong work ethic and a deep sense of responsibility, often going above and beyond to ensure his team had the resources and support they needed to succeed. While admirable, this dedication led to a tendency to shoulder excessive responsibilities, making it challenging for him to effectively delegate tasks or set healthy boundaries. Consequently, he frequently found himself overwhelmed, juggling multiple projects and deadlines, and struggling to maintain a sustainable workload.

My coaching focused on supporting him in developing strategies for better workload management and fostering a more balanced approach to his responsibilities. A key area was empowering him to confidently decline additional tasks when his capacity was reached and to proactively seek assistance from colleagues or supervisors when necessary. Another crucial aspect was enhancing his communication skills, particularly in the areas of transparency and constructive feedback. Encouraging open and honest dialogue within his team was seen as vital for building trust, identifying potential challenges early on, and fostering a collaborative environment where team members felt comfortable raising concerns and offering solutions. He learned techniques for delivering feedback that was both direct and supportive, focusing on specific behaviors and their impact, while also acknowledging individual strengths and contributions. His primary motivators were the successful completion of projects and the professional growth of his team members, which I leveraged by framing workload management and delegation not as relinquishing control, but as empowering his team and creating opportunities for their development. My role involved consistent support, active listening, and gentle nudges to encourage the implementation of new strategies. It was important to create a safe and nonjudgmental space where he felt comfortable exploring his challenges and experimenting with new approaches. Regular check-ins and accountability measures helped him stay on track and reinforce positive changes in his behavior, ultimately aiming to mitigate the risk of burnout and foster a more sustainable and fulfilling work experience for both himself and his team.

Case Study 3: Building Confidence, Cultivating Strategy: Coaching a Rising Talent

The new HR Business Partner demonstrated a strong desire to succeed and possessed a meticulous approach to her work, which are valuable assets. However, her focus on granular details occasionally overshadowed the broader strategic objectives of her role. Given that the position was both new to her and inherently complex, a structured approach to onboarding and ongoing support was implemented. This included the provision of comprehensive instructions for all assigned tasks and responsibilities and the opportunity to discuss her questions to ensure she felt confident in the assignment. Eventually, the high-touch support was scaled back as her confidence grew. To proactively address potential challenges and ensure continuous development, regular and scheduled check-in meetings were established. These meetings were to discuss any emerging issues, provide thorough answers to her inquiries, and deliver consistent and constructive feedback regarding her performance and progress. Furthermore, targeted efforts were made to cultivate her understanding of the interconnectedness between her daily activities and the overarching strategic goals of the organization. I then partnered her with a more senior member of the team for peer mentoring, which helped give her the space to talk through her concerns and questions. When she encountered obstacles or expressed feeling overwhelmed by the intricacies of specific tasks, support was readily available to help her regain perspective and reprioritize. Building her confidence was also a key focus, which was achieved through the consistent acknowledgment of her accomplishments and the reinforcement of her positive contributions. The overarching objective of this comprehensive support strategy was two-fold: to facilitate her mastery of her immediate responsibilities and to simultaneously foster the development of her strategic thinking capabilities for future growth and increased impact within the HR function.

The results of this personalized and relationship-centered coaching approach were transformative. As individuals felt seen, understood, and supported, their confidence and performance levels increased significantly. They became more proactive, took greater initiative, and demonstrated a stronger commitment to their work and the team's success. This positive individual growth, in turn, created a powerful ripple effect, contributing to a more collaborative, innovative, and high-performing team environment. The experience underscored that investing time and effort in understanding and connecting with each employee as an individual is not just a matter of good management but a fundamental driver of both individual and collective success.

From the HR Deck: The Tools of Tailored Coaching

As a manager, getting to know your people is the heart of situational coaching. But from my seat in HR, I know that leaving this entirely to intuition can be inconsistent. That's why we build systems and provide tools—not to replace a manager's judgment, but to give it a strategic starting point.

Two of the most powerful, and often misunderstood, tools in our toolkit are personality assessments and Individual Development Plans (IDPs).

*Let's be honest—personality assessments like DiSC or CliftonStrengths can sometimes feel like corporate horoscopes. It's tempting to see them as a fun, one-off team-building exercise and then forget about them. But that's a huge missed opportunity. From an HR perspective, these assessments are not meant to put people in a box; they are designed to be powerful **conversation starters**.*

When a manager understands that one team member is highly analytical and needs data to feel confident in a decision, while another is a natural collaborator who thrives on brainstorming, they can tailor their coaching approach. The assessment gives the manager a cheat sheet for how to best communicate, motivate, and delegate to each person on their team. It's the ultimate tool for practicing situational coaching at scale.

Similarly, the Individual Development Plan (IDP) can feel like just another piece of bureaucratic paperwork. But a great coach sees it for what it is: a formal, co-created roadmap for an employee's aspirations. It's the place where you document that your "go-getter" wants to lead a project by the end of the year, or that your "rising talent" wants to gain more confidence in presenting to senior leaders.

As an HR leader, my job is to provide these tools. But it's the manager on the ground, the one having the day-to-day coaching conversations, who brings them to life. When used effectively, these systems are the invisible infrastructure that turns a manager's good intentions into a consistent and equitable coaching practice for their entire team.

Understanding Generational Viewpoints on Feedback

Just as you adapt your coaching to individual personalities and career stages, understanding generational differences in how feedback is typically received can significantly enhance your effectiveness. It's crucial to remember that these are generalizations and that individual experiences within each generation can vary widely. However, understanding these broader trends can help managers tailor their feedback approach for maximum effectiveness. (And yes, for those wondering, Generation X very much exists and contributes!)

- Generation X (Born roughly 1965–1980):
  - **Feedback Experience:** Gen X often grew up with less frequent, more formal feedback, like annual or semiannual performance reviews. Many experienced a "sink or swim" mentality in their early careers.
  - **Viewpoint:** Gen Xers might be less accustomed to receiving regular feedback, so when it comes, they may be surprised or even unsettled. Gen X's feedback perspective is deeply rooted in their professional upbringing during a time of corporate

downsizing and less formal mentorship. They value competence and efficiency and view work as a transactional relationship: "I do my job well, and I expect autonomy and fair compensation in return." Because they weren't conditioned to expect frequent praise or check-ins, they may see it as a sign of distrust or an unnecessary distraction from the task at hand. Micromanagement is the ultimate sign of disrespect for their independence. When providing feedback, they are most receptive to a no-nonsense, direct approach that gets straight to the point and respects their time.

- ○ They may interpret feedback as indicating a problem or mistake rather than an opportunity for growth, particularly if it's not delivered carefully. They might be more comfortable with direct, concise feedback but less receptive to overly emotional or lengthy discussions. They value independence and competence and may feel micromanaged or questioned if feedback is too frequent or prescriptive.
- ○ **Coaching Approach:** Be clear, concise, and direct in your feedback. Avoid beating around the bush. Frame feedback as an opportunity for improvement, not just a critique. Provide specific examples and focus on behaviors rather than personality. Be respectful of their experience and independence. Allow them space to implement feedback in their own way. Don't assume they're seeking constant affirmation; occasional, thoughtful feedback is often more effective.
- ○ **Specific Coaching Example**: Instead of a daily check-in, a manager can say, "I'd like to schedule a quick 15-minute chat every two weeks to touch base on the progress of Project X. This will help us both stay aligned." This respects their autonomy and signals trust.
- • **Millennials/Generation Y (Born roughly 1981–1996):**
  - ○ **Feedback Experience:** Millennials grew up with more structured feedback, from teachers to coaches to parents. They often received praise and recognition for their efforts. Many experienced a "participation trophy" culture. Millennials grew up with a different educational model that emphasized

continuous assessment and collaborative projects. This translated into a desire for constant development and a clear sense of purpose at work. They don't just want to know *what* they're doing; they want to know *why* it matters and how it helps them grow. Feedback is not a punishment but a roadmap for their career progression. When feedback is sparse, they may interpret it as a lack of investment in their future. They respond best to a balance of positive reinforcement and constructive criticism.

- **Viewpoint:** Millennials generally expect and value feedback, both positive and constructive. They see it as a tool for development and growth. They appreciate frequent check-ins and ongoing communication. They may feel overlooked or undervalued if feedback is sparse. They respond well to feedback that is not only encouraging and supportive but also honest and direct. They appreciate understanding the "why" behind the feedback and how it connects to their personal and professional goals.
- **Coaching Approach:** Provide regular feedback, both informal and formal. Make it a part of your ongoing communication. Be specific and explain how their performance aligns with goals and expectations. Offer a balance of positive reinforcement and constructive criticism. Connect feedback to their development plans and career aspirations. Be open to their feedback and input on your coaching style.
- **Specific Coaching Example**: After a project milestone, a manager can say, "Great work on hitting that deadline. What's one thing you feel you learned from this process that you can take with you to the next project?" This links their performance to their personal growth.

- **Generation Z (Born roughly 1997–2012):**
  - **Feedback Experience:** Gen Z has grown up in a world of constant communication, instant feedback (social media, gaming), and personalized learning. They're accustomed to rapid iteration and quick adjustments. Gen Z lives in a world of constant digital feedback, from "likes" on social media to immediate

data in online gaming. They expect authenticity and transparency and are adept at spotting anything that feels "fake." For them, feedback should be immediate, specific, and tied directly to impact. They are less interested in formal, top-down reviews and more interested in real-time, two-way dialogue. They value a leader who is a partner in their learning, not just a boss

- **Viewpoint:** Gen Z expects immediate, frequent, and transparent feedback. They're used to getting feedback in real-time. They are highly tech-savvy and comfortable with receiving feedback through various digital platforms. They value authenticity and honesty. They're less likely to respond to inauthentic praise or sugar-coated criticism. They want to understand the impact of their work and how it contributes to the bigger picture.

- **Coaching Approach:** Provide real-time feedback whenever possible. Use digital tools and apps to make feedback easily accessible. Be direct and transparent. Avoid ambiguity or corporate jargon. Focus on impact and purpose. Explain how their work matters and how they can make a difference. Be open to two-way feedback. Gen Z wants to give feedback as much as they receive it. Recognize and reward their contributions frequently and publicly, especially in online spaces where they're active.

- **Specific Coaching Example**: Instead of waiting for a formal meeting, a manager can send a quick message after a presentation: "Just watched your client demo. The way you explained the new feature was really clear and confident. That's a huge step forward from last month! Keep it up." This is real-time, specific, and authentic.

- **Important Considerations for Managers:**
  - **Avoid Stereotypes:** These are general trends, not absolute rules. Get to know your individual team members and their preferences.
  - **Communicate Expectations:** Be upfront about your feedback style and ask employees about their preferences.
  - **Be Adaptable:** Adjust your approach based on the individual, the situation, and the specific feedback being given.

- ○ **Create a Feedback Culture:** Normalize feedback as a regular part of work. Encourage open communication, constructive dialogue, and a growth mindset.
- ○ **Provide Training:** Offer training on giving and receiving feedback for both managers and employees.

Coaching Challenge	What to Do (the Skill)	How to Do It (the Action)
Giving Feedback	Adapt the Frequency and Tone	For a Gen X employee, provide feedback less frequently but more directly, often in a scheduled 1:1. For a Millennial or Gen Z employee, make it a continuous, informal process.
Building Trust	Show, Don't Just Tell	For Gen X, build trust by giving them a task and stepping back, showing you trust their competence. For Millennials and Gen Z, build trust by being transparent about your own learning and struggles.
Connecting Work to Purpose	Explain the "Why"	For all generations, but especially for Millennials and Gen Z, explicitly state how a task contributes to the team's and company's mission. This is the difference between a task and a calling.
Promoting Psychological Safety	Invite Two-Way Dialogue	A manager's job is not just to give feedback but also to receive it. Ask your team, "What could I do to be a more effective coach for you?" This shows vulnerability and models the behavior you want to see.

All Generations Benefit from a Coach's Mindset

While understanding generational nuances is a valuable skill, it's not the ultimate solution. The most important lesson is that all generations benefit from the same core coaching principles: clear communication, genuine care, and a focus on growth. A manager who leans into a coaching mindset—by asking powerful questions, actively listening, and framing every interaction as an opportunity for development—will be effective with every person on their team, regardless of their age. A great coach knows that at the end of the day, people are people.

Your Coaching Action Plan: Try This Today

- **Identify One Motivator:** Pick one team member and spend 5 minutes in your next conversation asking about their career goals or what truly energizes them at work.
- **Tailor Your Next Feedback:** Before your next feedback conversation, consider the individual's learning style (e.g., direct, collaborative) and how you can best adapt your delivery.
- **Frame Delegation as Empowerment:** The next time you delegate a task, explicitly state the "why" and "what" (outcome), and give them autonomy on the "how."
- **Check for Overwhelm:** Ask a team member who typically takes on a lot if they feel supported or if there's anything you can take off their plate.
- **Acknowledge a Small Win:** Publicly (or privately, if preferred) acknowledge a small, specific accomplishment from a team member who shows growth or initiative.

The Ripple from This Chapter: The power of personalization creates a current of engagement. Now that we know how to connect with each person, let's look at how to channel that energy toward our ultimate goal: leading in the gray, and fostering innovation. When you move beyond a one-size-fits-all approach, you create a powerful current of engagement. An employee who feels truly understood becomes more loyal and more willing to bring their whole self to work. This ability to see and leverage the unique strengths of every person on your team isn't just good management—it's the secret ingredient for unlocking creativity, especially when the path forward isn't clear.

CHAPTER 5

Coaching for Innovation— Leading in the Gray

We've just explored how situational coaching allows us to leverage the diverse strengths of our team. Now, we'll put that skill to the ultimate test. This chapter is a playbook for one of the most critical inflection points in modern business: the need to innovate when the path forward is unclear. In these moments of ambiguity, traditional, top-down management fails. It is the leader's ability to coach—and to draw out the unique potential of each team member—that becomes the essential tool for fostering the psychological safety required for creative risk-taking.

Opening Scene: "We Needed Everything"

A couple of weeks into my new role as Senior Manager of HR at Power-School, I still didn't have a work computer, e-mail access, or even a clear picture of the business landscape I'd just stepped into. I did, however, have a deadline: Our first acquisition was weeks from closing, and about 100 new employees would soon need to be onboarded into a system that didn't yet exist.

I had just joined the company—only two months after PowerSchool itself had been acquired by a private equity firm. I was also leading a brand-new HR team of four, all of us new to the company, and none of us with prior experience in a private equity-backed environment. We weren't just building the plane while flying it; we were manufacturing the bolts mid-air.

We had no employee handbook. No structured onboarding plan. No finalized benefit administration through our HRIS system. Our open enrollment setup was already behind. And Randi—one of my early team members—was managing carrier links and system logic while navigating unfamiliar platforms.

To make things more complex, I'd been pulled into acquisition planning meetings late, tasked with reviewing employment agreements, drafting separation packages, and conducting as much due diligence as humanly possible in a matter of days. The stakes were high, the timeline was tight, and the margin for error was razor-thin.

And my team? Smart, eager, but junior. New not just to each other but also to a culture of ambiguity and urgency. There was no time to micromanage, which candidly is not in my DNA. What I needed wasn't control—it was commitment. I had to rally them. Not by barking orders but by coaching clarity in the chaos.

So, I started asking questions:

- "What's one part of this onboarding process we can own by Friday?"
- "Who on the new employee list do we have the most data gaps on—and how can we fix those first?"
- "What would 'good enough for Day 1' look like, and how do we get there together?"

We made it happen. Onboarding happened. Systems went live. People were hired—some even rehired, thanks to one painful misstep where we let someone go, only to realize they were essential. Titles were corrected. Comp was recalibrated. We got it done—not flawlessly, but forward.

And then we reflected. We created checklists. Built templates. Held focus groups with newly acquired employees to ask what worked—and what didn't. I built a manager playbook for welcoming new team members after acquisition. And most importantly, we shifted our mindset from "responding to change" to coaching through it.

That first acquisition taught me something I've carried through every deal since: When everything is unclear, coaching becomes the anchor. Not because it gives people the answers but because it gives them the confidence to find their own.

Why Innovation Begins with Trust

Innovation doesn't start with ideas—it starts with safety. Not the padded-corner kind of safety but psychological safety: the belief that you won't be punished for having a new idea, for asking a hard question, or for saying, "I don't know."

Traditional management models are rooted in control—clear steps, predictable outcomes, top-down instruction. And those models can work in static environments. But innovation happens when the steps are missing. It lives in the gray space between what we know and what we're about to discover. And in that space, control stifles. Coaching unlocks.

In that first acquisition at PowerSchool, I didn't know everything—and I made that clear. Instead of giving my team a polished answer (because I didn't have one), I shared context, offered support, and asked them what they saw that I might be missing. My coaching didn't erase the uncertainty, but it gave them the permission—and the structure—to step into it with confidence. We didn't get everything perfect, but we grew more agile, more trusting, and more courageous because of it.

Coaching isn't passive. It's not saying, "Do whatever feels right." It's asking the right questions to help people uncover what could be right—and then standing beside them as they figure it out. It's reminding someone, "You don't have to be certain to be competent."

When people feel safe, they're more likely to take intelligent risks. To question outdated systems. To say, "What if we tried this instead?"

And when that becomes the norm—when teams know they're not going to be micromanaged into mediocrity—they begin to own their thinking in a different way. They stop seeking approval and start seeking possibility. Coaching becomes the conduit, and trust becomes the catalyst.

Coaching When the Path Is Fuzzy

There's a kind of leadership that thrives in clarity. But there's another kind—the one forged in the gray space between deadlines, decisions, and doubt. That's the space coaching was built for.

When I joined PowerSchool, I was supposed to bring answers. Instead, I brought questions. I was leading a new team through an acquisition I barely had a handle on myself, with incomplete information and shifting priorities. There wasn't a playbook. There wasn't even a page.

So, I led the only way I knew how: by turning toward curiosity instead of control. That moment challenged me to rewire my instincts. To trade certainty for co-creation. To hold space for emerging clarity rather than chase premature perfection.

Because when the path is fuzzy, coaching means showing up—not to give the answer but to make it safer to keep asking.

I started asking different questions:

- "What's one thing we do know?"
- "If we had to make progress today, where would we start?"
- "What feels risky—and what feels necessary?"

The team followed my lead—not because I gave perfect direction but because I gave them permission to think. I shared my own uncertainty out loud. I showed them that leadership doesn't mean having everything figured out—it means being willing to figure things out together.

There's a strange kind of magic that happens when a leader says, "I trust you to try."

People lean in. They take initiative. They begin to experiment. Not recklessly, but thoughtfully—because you've set the tone that failure isn't fatal, it's information.

In fact, we created a habit after that first acquisition: after-action reviews. What worked? What surprised us? What can we improve next time?

We didn't just recover from our mistakes. We metabolized them into muscle.

Coaching in the unknown means resisting the urge to protect your team from every mistake. It means anchoring them with values and direction—but not taking over the wheel every time the fog rolls in.

As leaders, we're not just guides through complexity. We're also mirrors. And when we reflect back someone's strengths, their instincts, their capacity to adapt—we help them see that clarity isn't a prerequisite for courage.

Coaching Habits That Spark Innovation

Innovation often grows best in soil that's been tilled with trust, not tension. And sometimes the simplest rituals have the biggest impact. You don't need flashy brainstorms or innovation sprints to build a creative culture—you need consistency, reflection, and moments where people feel seen.

Here are a few coaching-inspired micro-habits that helped my teams stretch, recover, and create—even in the messiest environments:

"Way to Go Wednesdays"

Every Wednesday, we carved out time to celebrate something. We called it Way to Go Wednesdays, and it didn't have to be groundbreaking—just genuine.

- Someone might share that they finally got their inbox under control.
- Another might mention finishing a complicated benefits audit.
- And sometimes, it was personal: a toddler slept through the night, a mom made it to her kid's soccer game.

In the midst of tight deadlines and constant change, this ritual created breathing room. It reminded us that we were human first, and that progress—no matter how small—is worth pausing for.

What I didn't fully realize until later was how Wednesday Wins laid the groundwork for innovation. When people feel safe celebrating effort and incremental progress, they're more likely to take initiative. They start suggesting better ways to do things. They ask smarter questions. They experiment—because they know we'll honor the attempt, not just the outcome.

Micro-Risks Check-In

Alongside wins, I started asking my team during our weekly 1:1s:

"What's one small risk you took this week?"

Sometimes it was about speaking up in a cross-functional meeting. Other times, it was trying out a new approach to onboarding or flagging a broken system no one had noticed. The habit wasn't about rewarding recklessness—it was about normalizing experimentation.

Our unspoken agreement became clear: You're allowed to stumble if you're willing to learn—and if we're willing to fix it together.

Reverse Debriefs

After every acquisition, our team didn't just celebrate what went right. We dissected what didn't—and we did it openly.

We'd ask:

- What did we overlook?
- What assumption broke down?
- What feedback surprised us from newly acquired employees?

But we didn't stop there—we fixed the process, not just the problem. Out of these moments came templates, playbooks, manager guides, and, most importantly, a culture that believed, "We can fix this."

That phrase became a quiet mantra. It meant you could move quickly because the support net was strong. It meant we prioritized learning loops over blame spirals. And it meant innovation wasn't a lightning bolt—it was an everyday practice.

From Coach to Culture Shaper

When people hear the word "culture," they often imagine sweeping vision statements, all-hands meetings, or HR-led engagement campaigns. But in reality, culture often begins at the team level—with micro-behaviors that get repeated, normalized, and eventually absorbed into "how we do things around here."

That's why coaching, when practiced consistently, doesn't just elevate individuals—it rewires the system.

In those early acquisition days at PowerSchool, we didn't have time to wait for perfect top-down alignment. But we could shape the experience of our own team, and the newly acquired employees joining us. Through coaching, we normalized a few key messages:

- Ask questions, even if they feel obvious.
- Celebrate progress, not just perfection.

- Share what broke—so we can build it back stronger.
- You don't need a title to offer an idea.

As those practices took hold, other teams began noticing. Managers who had never onboarded acquired employees before started asking for our playbooks. Leaders wanted access to the templates we'd built, or the check-in questions we used to support new hires. What started as a survival reflex—an instinct to coach instead of command—quietly became part of the company's acquisition muscle.

That's the quiet superpower of coaching. It doesn't just influence people. It influences patterns.

You can tell when a team has been coached. They interrupt each other less. They offer credit more freely. They ask stronger questions. They recover faster. Over time, those traits don't stay isolated—they spread.

Coaching becomes culture when people coach each other, even when you're not in the room.

And when that happens, your role as a leader begins to evolve. You stop being the conductor of every move. You become the architect of the environment—designing rhythms and rituals where trust, experimentation, and learning are built-in.

That's leadership at scale. Not just driving execution—but shaping belief.

Spotlight Story: Coaching Through Craig (the Other Craig)

If you want to know whether your leadership sticks, don't just look at the results you delivered. Look at the leaders you developed and what they do when they have a chance to lead others.

Craig was one of those people for me.

As the Senior Manager of Total Rewards on my team, Craig didn't just embrace a coaching mindset—he made it his strategy. While other managers often sought out polished, resume-ready candidates, Craig preferred something else entirely: interns. Entry-level hires. People with raw talent and untapped potential.

He didn't see inexperience as a liability. He saw it as an invitation.

"I can teach them the technical skills," he once told me. "What I care about is their curiosity—the way they think, how they treat people, and whether they're open to growing."

That was classic Craig. He built his team not by plugging in finished products but by shaping future leaders. He gave his people space to explore, tools to succeed, and the safety to get things wrong along the way.

And he didn't just say he was a coach—he showed it:

- He spent time understanding how each team member learned best.
- He offered regular feedback, always framed with respect and optimism.
- He challenged people—but never without support.

One of the things I appreciated most was how Craig's approach echoed the very things I'd tried to model with him: ownership, emotional intelligence, and a fierce belief in people's potential.

His team noticed. They took risks. They initiated ideas. They spoke up, even when they weren't sure they were "ready." They didn't wait for permission—they carried their permission with them.

And just like that, the wave continued.

One day, after a particularly complex project rollout, one of his newest team members expressed worry about a system glitch they'd overlooked. Craig didn't panic. He smiled and said:

"Don't stress—we can fix anything that goes wrong."

That's coaching. Not blind optimism, but grounded reassurance. Not ignoring problems, but choosing learning over blame. That phrase, quietly offered, told his team everything they needed to know: We've got this. Together.

The Leader You Become in the Process

Coaching for innovation doesn't just change your team—it changes you. It rewires how you think, how you lead, and how you respond when the ground shifts beneath your feet.

I used to think leadership meant having the answers. That the best way to support my team was to protect them from risk, anticipate every curveball, and hand them polished solutions. But in those first few acquisition rollouts—when information was incomplete and timelines were tight—I realized something powerful:

Leadership Isn't About Control. It's About Courage

Courage to pause before reacting. Courage to admit you're unsure. Courage to see someone's potential before they see it themselves.

There were moments in those early days when I quietly questioned whether we'd get it all done. Whether I was asking too much. Whether the missteps would overshadow the effort. But then someone on my team would step up with an insight I hadn't considered. They'd catch an error. They'd fix the glitch. They'd surprise me.

And over time, I learned to stop trying to carry everything alone. I stopped rescuing. I started trusting—and in that trust, I watched people become who they didn't yet know they could be.

That's the gift of coaching. It asks you to lead not with ego, but with invitation. Not with perfection, but with presence.

Now, when I meet uncertainty, I don't tighten my grip. I ask better questions. I give people space to find their footing. I remind myself—and them of this simple truth:

"We can fix anything that goes wrong. As long as we're learning."

Because in the end, innovation doesn't require fearlessness. It requires faith. And coaching? Coaching builds that faith—one conversation, one question, one ripple at a time.

Innovation Isn't a Lightning Bolt. It's a Ripple.

Innovation rarely arrives fully formed. It doesn't crash down in a moment of brilliance—it unfolds through the quiet courage of people willing to try, to trust, and to grow. And coaching is what makes that courage sustainable.

You don't need to be a product visionary or a Fortune 500 CEO to lead innovation. You just need to ask the right questions, build safety through trust, and create the conditions where creativity can breathe.

In times of uncertainty, people don't need your perfection—they need your presence. Your belief in them. Your invitation to think boldly and your promise to stand beside them if things break.

Because the most powerful force in a culture of innovation isn't strategy.

It's a leader who coaches.

Inflection Point Playbook: Fostering Innovation on Your Team

- Launch with a Question, Not a Plan: Instead of presenting a fully formed idea, present a compelling problem. Frame the challenge with a powerful question like, "How might we solve X for our customers in a way no one else has?" This creates a sense of ownership from the start.
- Schedule "Safe-to-Fail" Sprints: Dedicate specific, time-boxed periods for experimentation where the explicit goal is learning, not a perfect outcome. This lowers the stakes and encourages creative risk-taking.
- Coach for Curiosity: During 1:1s, shift the focus from "What did you accomplish?" to "What did you learn?" and "What surprised you this week?" This reinforces that discovery is a valued part of the process.
- Publicly Celebrate "Intelligent Failures": When a well-intentioned experiment doesn't work, discuss it openly in a team meeting. Express gratitude to the person for taking the risk and lead a discussion on the valuable lessons learned. This is the most powerful way to cultivate psychological safety.

The Ripple from This Chapter

The ripple from this chapter is one of courage—both for your team and for you. Coaching for innovation means creating the psychological safety for your team to take intelligent risks. But what builds safety and trust isn't universal. The very behaviors that make a team member in one office feel safe to speak up might make a colleague across the world feel uncomfortable. To truly unlock the innovative potential of a diverse team, we must first understand how to adapt our coaching to their unique cultural contexts.

Your Coaching Action Plan—Do This Today

Use these questions to deepen your practice as an innovation coach—whether you're leading a team, a project, or simply yourself:

- What's one area in your work where you could trade control for curiosity?
- When was the last time you celebrated a micro-win? Who on your team could use that celebration this week?
- How do you respond when something breaks—do you punish, or do you ask, "What did we learn?"
- What "permission slip" could you offer your team right now to help them take a risk?
- And finally…
- What's one coaching ripple you've started—intentionally or not—that's still moving outward today?

CHAPTER 6

Coaching Across Cultures— Leading with Global Intelligence

In the last chapter, we established that psychological safety is the bedrock of innovation. But how do we build that safety when our team spans multiple countries, cultures, and communication styles? What feels like direct, honest feedback in one culture can feel blunt and disrespectful in another. This chapter is about developing our global intelligence as coaches, learning to adapt our approach to ensure our message is not just heard, but felt, no matter where our team members are.

Opening Reflection: Coaching Doesn't Always Translate

One of the earliest lessons I learned about cross-cultural coaching came from a call with my team in India.

At the time, I was leading a global HR function that spanned Canada, India, and across the United States. My style had always worked well: calm, direct, and focused—clear without being pushy. I've never been the "stress about the small stuff" type of leader. I like to keep things moving, give people space to work, and keep communication honest and productive.

But during this particular project, something was off. My India-based team members kept agreeing to deliverables in meetings, but by the following week, nothing had moved forward. At first, I thought maybe I hadn't been clear—so I clarified. Still nothing. Then I added more detail to what I needed, broke it into next steps, and asked for confirmation.

Still… silence when it came to execution.

That's when it finally clicked: It wasn't a comprehension issue. It was a comfort issue. They didn't feel they had the space to tell me something wasn't working.

I'd been moving through meetings in my usual West Coast rhythm—polite but efficient, no fluff, no pressure. But for my team, that tone was missing something essential: warmth, rapport, an invitation to open up.

I hadn't realized that skipping the small talk—checking in on family, sharing updates from my side, asking how things were going outside of the project—meant I was also skipping the trust. I wasn't giving them the safety to say, "Actually, we're running into issues," or "Here's what we need help with."

So, I shifted. I slowed down and opened our meetings with space for connection—how was the weekend, how are your parents, what's new in your world? I shared more from my side, too—not out of obligation but because that's how relationships are built. I also learned to ask better questions. Not just, "Is this on track?" but "Is there anything in the way I can help remove?"

And they responded beautifully. That team became one of the most engaged, thoughtful, and hardworking groups I've had the privilege to lead.

It taught me what no training ever could: Coaching across cultures isn't just about what you say. It's about how you say it, when you say it, and whether the people on the other end feel safe enough to answer honestly.

Why Culture Shapes Coaching

Coaching isn't just about intention. It's about interpretation. And interpretation lives in culture. When we think of "culture," we often default to nationality or geography. But in coaching, culture shows up in countless ways: regional norms, generational values, company history, even team dynamics. It's the invisible language underneath what's being said—the emotional code that shapes how feedback lands, how questions are heard, and how safety is built.

That's why two people can receive the exact same coaching conversation—same words, same delivery—and walk away with entirely different experiences. One feels empowered. The other, unsettled. Culture is the lens they're looking through.

In my own leadership journey, I've coached and managed teams in South Africa, India, Australia, Canada, Ukraine, the UK, Kosovo, and across every U.S. time zone. And what I've learned—sometimes the hard way—is that what's "clear" to me isn't always clear to them. What feels "respectful" in one place might feel evasive or abrupt in another. Not because anyone is wrong but because the meaning isn't just in the message—it's in the context.

A colleague on the East Coast might appreciate jumping right into the action items. My team in India, however, wanted to first hear about how my weekend was. They'd share family updates, weather reports, snippets of everyday life—and they wanted the same from me. It wasn't a detour. It was the doorway.

Coaching across cultures starts with this simple truth: Relationship comes before results.

That doesn't mean sacrificing performance or watering down feedback. It means customizing your approach so that it's heard the way you mean it to be heard. And that requires something deeper than competence—it takes cultural humility.

Because even when we coach with the best of intentions, it's not our words that build trust—it's our willingness to listen, adjust, and learn.

Coaching Through Context: High Versus Low Communication Cultures

If coaching is a conversation, then context is its grammar.

In global leadership, the way people give, receive, and even expect communication can vary wildly—and much of it traces back to whether a culture is high-context or low-context. Understanding this difference can dramatically improve how coaching is delivered across borders, and it explains why your carefully framed feedback might resonate in one country and completely miss in another.

High-Context Versus Low-Context, Defined

Coined by anthropologist Edward T. Hall, the concept of high-context and low-context communication describes how much a culture relies on shared understanding, relationships, and unspoken norms to convey meaning.

Style	High-Context Cultures	Low-Context Cultures
Examples	Japan, India, UAE, China, Latin America	U.S., Germany, Scandinavia, Australia, Canada (varies)
Communication	Indirect, layered with nuance	Direct, explicit, "say what you mean"
Interpretation	Meaning depends on tone, relationship, shared history	Meaning depends on the actual words used
Feedback	Often implied or softened to maintain harmony	Given directly, even if critical
Decision Making	Relationship-based, consensus valued	Task-based, individual ownership emphasized

Neither approach is right or wrong—just different. But when coaching across these contexts, the risk isn't just miscommunication—it's misconnection.

Coaching Across the Divide

When I worked with my India-based team, I encountered this cultural contrast firsthand. In my West Coast style—clear, calm, and results-oriented—I assumed that asking, "Are we good with that timeline?" was enough. In reality, for them to feel comfortable answering honestly, I needed to create a more relational opening and offer them graceful ways to raise concerns without feeling like they were letting me down.

In high-context cultures, direct feedback—especially in front of others—can feel shaming or confrontational. People may nod or agree to maintain harmony, not because they don't have concerns but because the space hasn't been made safe enough to express them.

In contrast, in low-context cultures, withholding feedback or being overly indirect might appear evasive or passive. A manager might assume alignment when, in fact, no one is on the same page.

As coaches and leaders, we need to shift the way we ask questions and read responses:

- Replace "Why didn't this get done?" with "Is there anything in the way I can help with?"
- Instead of "Do you agree?," try "What concerns might you have that we haven't addressed yet?"
- Don't just listen to words—listen to what's missing, to hesitations, to tone, to body language.

From the HR Deck: Calibrating Performance Across Cultures
Once a year, in conference rooms all over the corporate world, a high-stakes ritual takes place: the performance calibration meeting. This is where managers gather to discuss their teams, debate ratings, and ultimately decide who gets the promotion, the bonus, or the spot on the high-potential list. From my seat in HR, this room is one of the most revealing places in the entire organization. It's where a manager's coaching skills—or lack thereof—have a direct and lasting impact on someone's career.

Now, imagine doing this for a global team.

On the screen, you have two employees up for the same promotion. One, from the U.S., speaks confidently about their accomplishments using "I" statements. Their manager presents a list of their impressive individual wins. The other employee, based in Japan, speaks with humility, emphasizing the team's collective success and using "we" statements. Their manager talks about their role as a great collaborator.

In a purely data-driven, culturally unaware room, who do you think gets the promotion? Too often, it's the person who is better at the game of self-promotion, not necessarily the person with the most potential.

This is the systemic challenge we face in HR. It's my job to ensure our talent processes are equitable, but I can't be in every conversation. This is where the manager as a culturally fluent coach becomes the most critical player in the room.

A great coach knows how to translate. They can say, "I know Hiroshi is using 'we' language, but let me tell you about the specific role he played in leading that project to success. In his culture, claiming individual credit would be seen as arrogant, but make no mistake, he was the driver."

Without that coaching and cultural translation from their manager, Hiroshi's potential gets lost in translation. A manager who understands this doesn't just advocate for their employee; they protect the integrity of the entire talent system. They ensure that potential is seen and valued, regardless of the cultural package it comes in.

Adapting Coaching Tools Across Cultures

Cultural agility doesn't mean lowering standards—it means finding the right bridge. It means being intentional about how safety is built. It means learning to say the same message differently, so that it lands with impact and respect.

Because coaching isn't just about performance. It's about belonging. And when people feel understood, they're not just willing to follow—they're ready to lead.

Cultural fluency isn't about having the perfect playbook for every region—it's about listening closely enough to adjust your approach without losing your intention. It's choosing curiosity over assumption. And it's recognizing that, in coaching, how you frame the message matters just as much as the message itself.

In a coaching conversation, every element carries meaning: your tone, your timing, your word choice, even your metaphors. In one culture, a sports analogy might spark motivation. In another, it might fall flat—or miss entirely.

To coach effectively across cultures, it's not about throwing out your tools. It's about modifying your grip.

Ask Before You Act: Framing for Clarity

One of the most powerful (and underused) questions when coaching someone from a different cultural background is:

"How do you prefer to receive feedback?"

It's simple. It's respectful. And it gives you immediate insight into how to coach with context.

Some individuals prefer a candid, bullet-point approach. Others may value a warmer lead-in or even a separate follow-up meeting to reflect first. For some, constructive feedback must begin with strengths. Others may want the bottom-line up front, no sugarcoating.

Another great one:

"What helps you feel most supported when you're stuck?"

That's coaching—in partnership, not assumption.

Reframing Common Coaching Tools

Let's say you're using a standard model like GROW. It's proven and widely applicable—but how you phrase each section can soften or clarify your tone.

Coaching Phase	Western Framing (Direct)	Adapted for High-Context Cultures
Goal	"What's your objective?"	"What would success look like to you in this?"
Reality	"What's blocking you?"	"What's made this challenging so far?"
Options	"What could you do differently?"	"What are some possible next steps we could explore together?"
Will	"What's your next action?"	"What feels like the right next move for you?"

It's not about diluting accountability. It's about creating safety for honesty.

Metaphors Matter

A well-placed metaphor can spark clarity—but only when it resonates.

- Don't assume everyone has a shared cultural frame of reference (e.g., American football, baseball analogies, or idioms like "hit it out of the park").
- Test metaphors gently and be ready to pivot. Storytelling is more universal than sports—consider personal analogies, nature imagery, or shared professional experiences.
- Even phrases like "radical candor" might need explanation—some cultures interpret "radical" quite differently.

When in doubt, ask:

"Does that metaphor land for you?" "Is there a better way to describe it in your world?"

That alone builds connection.

Coaching by Listening, Not Just Leading

Coaching across cultures begins when we stop assuming we're the most fluent person in the room. Instead of asking ourselves "How do I lead this coaching session well?," the better question might be:

"How can I learn enough about this person to make them feel seen?"

Sometimes the real coaching breakthrough isn't a brilliant question—it's the humility to say, "What does support look like for you right now?"

Coaching Across Languages and Time Zones

The modern team isn't always in the same building—or even the same hemisphere. We don't just lead across borders now; we coach across bandwidths. And while technology helps bridge the distance, it doesn't remove the human nuance. If anything, it magnifies it.

Coaching virtually or across languages challenges us to be even more intentional with how we build trust, create connection, and make space for nuance. But it also offers a powerful opportunity: to show up as a steady presence, even when we're not in the room.

Time Zones Create Power Dynamics

When half your team is starting their day while the other half is logging off, equity gets complicated. Are you always asking one region to stay late? Are people in certain time zones missing live coaching moments? Does your calendar reflect respect—or convenience?

As a leader, I always tried to rotate call times, share detailed recaps, and offer asynchronous coaching support. Whether it was a recorded Loom, a thoughtful Slack check-in, or a bulleted follow-up e-mail, I wanted my team to feel supported even if they couldn't join live. Because coaching isn't just in the meetings—it's in the moments we remember to include people on the edges.

Language Isn't the Barrier—Assumption Is

English might be the working language, but fluency isn't always equal. And coaching—nuanced, emotional, reflexive—is often the first place where that gap shows up.

If I noticed hesitation or vague agreement in a meeting, I didn't assume confusion. I assumed I needed to create clarity. I started speaking with fewer idioms, avoided "loaded" metaphors like "throwing someone under the bus," and made sure I left room between questions and answers. Silence wasn't awkward—it was generosity.

Tools that helped:

- Shared meeting notes with bolded questions and action items
- Visuals (slides, diagrams, workflows) to anchor the message
- Direct but warm questions like, "Was anything I said unclear or too fast?"

That wasn't dumbing anything down. It was lifting communication up to meet people with dignity.

Show Presence When You're Not Physically Present

Coaching doesn't need to be synchronous to be supportive. Some of my most effective coaching happened through:

- Thoughtful, timely e-mail feedback that named a strength and a growth edge
- Voice messages that offered encouragement after a tough meeting
- A Slack DM checking in—not about a task but about a person's energy

These "digital coaching touches" may be small, but when repeated, they build consistency. And consistency builds safety.

When you lead across geography, coaching becomes a study in generosity: generous listening, generous clarity, and generous trust. The goal isn't perfect communication. It's intentional connection. Because when people feel seen across miles and languages—that's when global coaching becomes global belonging.

Building a Global Coaching Culture

Creating a truly global coaching culture isn't achieved through training slides or policy PDFs. It happens through intentional modeling—one leader, one conversation, and one delightful ripple at a time.

Whether you're leading across borders or coaching across departments, here's what it takes to embed inclusive, culturally fluent coaching at scale:

Train Leaders to Ask, Not Assume

Most coaching breakdowns aren't caused by malice; they're caused by good intentions moving too fast. That's why the first muscle every global leader must build is inquiry. As HR leaders, it's essential to foster a culture where asking the right questions is valued over having all the answers. This approach not only prevents misunderstandings but also encourages a deeper connection and trust between leaders and their teams. By prioritizing inquiry, we create an environment where employees feel heard and understood, paving the way for meaningful growth and development.

Instead of training people what to say, teach them to ask:

- "What makes feedback feel useful to you?"
- "In your past work cultures, what did great support look like?"
- "Is there anything about how we communicate that could work better for you?"

These aren't just "nice" questions. They're strategic. They build coaching fluency by centering the experience of the person being coached—not the ego of the person delivering it.

Let Employee Voices Shape the Approach

One of the most overlooked sources of coaching excellence? The people you're coaching.

Ask for feedback on your own coaching regularly and make space for anonymous responses. Partner with Employee Resource Groups (ERGs), regional leaders, or cross-cultural advocates to understand how different communities experience feedback, trust, and leadership. Let their insights shape your development programs and management playbooks.

Because a global coaching culture isn't built on people—it's built with them.

Normalize Feedback Diversity

In some cultures, a moment of silence means disagreement. In others, it signifies deep respect. Teach your teams that feedback won't always look the same—and that's not a problem to fix. It's a pattern to explore. Create psychological safety not just for speaking up, but for speaking differently. Give managers the tools to distinguish between "quiet resistance" and "thoughtful processing." Promote empathy, not uniformity. This doesn't dilute coaching effectiveness—it deepens it.

As HR leaders, it's crucial to recognize that cultural nuances play a significant role in communication. By fostering an environment where diverse expressions of feedback are understood and valued, we can build stronger, more inclusive teams. Encourage managers to engage in active listening and to ask clarifying questions when faced with silence. This approach not only enhances understanding but also builds trust and respect within the team. Remember, the goal is not to create a homogeneous culture but to celebrate and leverage the richness of diverse perspectives. This way, we can truly harness the power of coaching to drive innovation and growth.

Anchor in Values, Not Scripts

When coaching across cultures, values create the common ground that language sometimes can't. Clarity. Respect. Growth. Trust. If your leaders understand why they're coaching, they're more likely to find the how, even when the path looks different. Encourage teams to adapt language, tone, or structure to fit regional nuance, as long as it aligns with your shared leadership philosophy. That flexibility turns coaching from a technique into a living, breathing practice. A coaching culture isn't built by perfect conversations. It's built by courageous consistency.

As HR leaders, it's essential to recognize that cultural diversity enriches the coaching experience. By fostering an environment where values are the cornerstone, we can bridge the gaps that language might create. Encourage your leaders to embrace regional nuances and adapt their coaching methods accordingly. This approach not only respects cultural differences but also strengthens the connection between leaders and their teams. Remember, the goal is to create a coaching culture that thrives on flexibility and authenticity. It's not about having flawless conversations; it's about consistently showing up with courage and commitment. This way, we can build a truly global coaching culture that drives performance and growth.

Coaching for True Inclusion and Belonging

Beyond cultural nuances and communication styles, a truly human-centered coaching culture actively champions inclusion and belonging. This isn't just about "checking a box" for diversity; it's about leveraging coaching as a powerful tool to ensure every voice is heard, valued, and empowered to contribute fully. For an INFJ leader, like me, this resonates deeply with the desire for fairness and seeing the unseen potential in everyone. Similarly, an ENFP might find joy in the creative possibilities of coaching, while an ISTJ would appreciate the structured approach to achieving goals. Each personality type brings its unique strengths to the table, making the coaching culture richer and more dynamic

Here's how coaching fosters genuine inclusion and belonging:

- **Actively Seek Out Quiet Voices:** Some team members, due to personality, cultural background, or past experiences, may be less inclined to speak up in meetings or offer dissenting opinions. A coaching leader intentionally creates space for these voices.

- ○ *Coaching Action:* After a meeting, follow up with individuals who were quiet: "I noticed you were thoughtful in the meeting today. Did anything come to mind that you didn't get a chance to share?" or "I value your perspective; is there a different way you'd prefer to share your ideas in team settings?"
- **Challenge Assumptions and Unconscious Bias (Your Own and Others'):** We all carry biases. A coaching mindset encourages self-awareness and gentle inquiry to uncover them.
  - ○ *Coaching Action:* When you notice a pattern (e.g., certain ideas always coming from the same demographic, or someone being consistently interrupted), coach yourself first: "Am I giving everyone equal airtime?" Then, you might coach others: "I noticed we heard a lot from X and Y today. What are ways we can ensure we're hearing from everyone on the team?" or "When Z shared their idea, it seemed to get less traction. What do we need to do to fully explore all ideas?"
- **Coach for Psychological Safety in Micro-Moments:** Reinforce that it's safe to make mistakes, ask "dumb" questions, or challenge the status quo. This is especially crucial for those from underrepresented groups who may feel higher stakes.
  - ○ *Coaching Action:* When someone takes a risk or admits an error, immediately reinforce the learning: "Thank you for raising that; what did we learn from it?" or "I appreciate you speaking up. That's exactly the kind of candid feedback we need to improve."
- **Tailor Development to Diverse Paths:** Recognize that career paths and growth aspirations may look different for individuals from varied backgrounds.
  - ○ *Coaching Action:* Instead of imposing a single career ladder, ask: "What does success look like for *you*?" "What unique strengths do you bring that we can leverage?" "How can I support your growth in a way that aligns with your personal and professional values?"
- **Champion Equity in Opportunities:** Coaching leaders are attuned to ensuring equitable access to stretch assignments, visibility, and mentorship.

◦ *Coaching Action:* Proactively identify opportunities for diverse team members to lead projects, present to senior leaders, or connect with mentors. "I see your strength in X; I think you'd be a great fit for this new project. Would you be interested in leading it?"

By weaving these inclusive coaching practices into the daily fabric of leadership, you don't just create a diverse team; you create a truly belonging team. It's where every individual feels empowered to bring their whole, authentic self to work, knowing their unique contributions are not just accepted, but celebrated. This is where the ripple effect of human potential truly reaches its fullest, most vibrant expression.

The Ripple from This Chapter: The ripple from this chapter is one of belonging. When you adapt your coaching style to be culturally fluent, your team members feel respected and understood, not just as employees but as individuals. This skill of adapting your approach with empathy is crucial. Now, we will take that same skill and apply it not just to different cultures but also to the most critical and emotionally charged moments of an employee's career: the personal and professional inflection points that define their journey.

Your Coaching Action Plan: Try This Today

You've learned that a coaching culture is about belonging, and that starts with cultural fluency. Here are five actions you can take today to build trust and connect with your team across different communication styles.

- **Start with Small Talk.** In your next virtual meeting, don't jump straight to the agenda. Spend the first 2 minutes genuinely checking in with your team. Ask about their weekend or how things are going outside of the project.
- **Ask for Feedback Preferences.** In your next one-on-one with a team member from a different cultural background, simply ask: "How do you prefer to receive feedback?" This shows respect and gives you the context you need to be an effective coach for them.

- **Listen for the Pause.** When you ask a question in a meeting, pay attention to the moments of silence. Instead of filling the space, give your team a few extra seconds to think and respond. That silence isn't awkward; it's an opportunity for thoughtfulness.
- **Audit Your Language.** Look at a recent e-mail you sent to a global team. Read it for idioms or metaphors that might not translate well. Next time, try to use more direct and universal language to ensure your message is clear and inclusive.
- **Offer Asynchronous Support.** Think about a team member in a different time zone. Send them a thoughtful check-in via chat or e-mail, not about a task but about their well-being. This small "digital coaching touch" builds consistency and reminds them you are present even when you're not physically there.

CHAPTER 7

Coaching at the Inflection Point—Navigating the Brave and the Broken

We have explored how to adapt our coaching for different personalities and global cultures. Now, we turn our focus to adapting our coaching for different moments. Life isn't a straight line; it's a series of inflection points—the unexpected promotion, the challenging project, the personal crisis. These are the moments where a leader's coaching matters most, where our presence can help navigate the brave and the broken.

From the HR Deck: The Re-Org Ripple

Nothing creates an inflection point faster than a reorganization. As an HR leader, I'm often one of the first to know. While leaders are focused on the new org chart, I'm focused on the human element. I immediately start coaching managers on the conversations they need to have. We role-play how to deliver the news with empathy, how to re-anchor the "survivors" to a new purpose, and how to manage the emotional fallout. A re-org isn't just a structural change; it's a series of deeply personal inflection points. My role is to build the coaching capability within the leadership team to navigate the human ripples the new structure will inevitably create.

We've explored how coaching anchors us through life's curveballs and breakthroughs. But even with the most supportive coach, there's one universal truth that often shifts uncomfortably once we leave the classroom and enter the cubicle: our relationship with feedback. Why does something so vital for growth suddenly feel so complicated?

Opening Scene: When the Curveball Comes

It wasn't on the calendar. It never is.

Maybe it's the layoff call. Or the job someone didn't land. The promotion they did get—but now feel completely unprepared for. The project that fell apart. The manager who left. The personal crisis is leaking into Zoom windows and inboxes.

These are the moments where coaching stops being developmental and becomes deeply human.

I remember one direct report—brilliant, driven, constantly outperforming. But after an unexpected reorg shifted their scope and removed a visible stretch assignment, they came to me and told me: "I'm trying, but it just doesn't feel like I matter here anymore."

They didn't need a pep talk. They didn't need productivity hacks. They needed space. Reflection. Clarity. And someone willing to meet them in the in-between.

That's what coaching at the inflection point demands: not just direction but devotion. Not just answers but accompaniment.

Recognizing When Coaching Needs to Shift

Most of us recognize disruption when it's visible—someone gets laid off, moved, promoted. But inflection points don't always come with a formal memo. They show up in subtle ways:

- A team member growing unusually quiet in meetings
- A performer suddenly second-guessing small decisions
- A new leader smiling on the outside but shrinking on the inside
- A previously engaged employee asking fewer questions

The moment may not be seismic on the org chart—but inside, it's shaking something loose.

This is when your role as a coach becomes both softer and sharper:

- Softer in listening, compassion, and permission
- Sharper in noticing shifts, naming what others won't, and offering anchoring questions

A few signs I've learned to watch for:

- Repetition of doubt-based language ("I don't want to screw this up…")
- Over-indexing on perfection or overwork
- Withdrawal from stretch conversations
- A hyperfocus on external validation ("Was that, okay?" "Did I do it right?")

When those moments arise, a leader has a choice: redirect or reconnect. Coaching at the inflection point starts with connection.

Coaching Through the Breakdown

Not every inflection is forward. Some moments feel like breaking. A lost job. A career setback. A misstep that turned public. A personal crisis bleeding into professional performance.

In those moments, your job isn't to fix it—it's to hold space for it. Here's what I've found helpful:

- Name the real, gently. "It seems like something shifted for you recently. Want to talk it through?"
- Normalize the spiral. "You're not broken. You're in motion. This discomfort is evidence of growth."
- Anchor to identity, not circumstance. "Regardless of role or title—what are your strengths showing you right now?"
- Ask, then pause. Silence is where reflection settles. Give them room.

One leader I coached went from leading a team of ten to suddenly being an IC after a reorg. Her words: "I feel like I failed."

What she didn't need: a rebuttal.

What she did need: to hear that her value wasn't tied to span of control, and that influence doesn't always wear a title.

We created a roadmap for reinvention—identifying her core leadership contributions, mapping what energized her, and setting near-term goals rooted in influence, not hierarchy.

Because coaching in the breakdown isn't just damage control. It's soul work.

A Case Study in Grace: How My Manager Coached Me Through a Crisis

I experienced this level of human-centered coaching firsthand from my own manager, Dawn, during one of the most challenging periods of my life. Dawn and I had worked closely together for several years, navigating many high-stakes, high-stress projects. We had a strong professional relationship built on mutual respect.

That relationship was truly tested at the start of the COVID-19 pandemic, when my son began to experience significant health issues of his own. The situation was not straightforward and demanded an enormous amount of my time, focus, and emotional energy. Feeling that transparency was the only way forward, I told Dawn exactly what was going on with my family.

Her response was the embodiment of coaching through a breakdown. There was no discussion of modified deadlines or concerns about my focus. Instead, she was simply, unequivocally, kind and understanding. She gave me the space and grace to do my best to balance everything when I needed to.

Because of her reaction, a layer of immense stress was lifted from my shoulders. I didn't have to worry about how my personal crisis was going to impact my job; I was able to focus on my son. Her empathy created a bubble of psychological safety at a time when the world felt anything but safe.

I know for a fact that plenty of bosses out there wouldn't have cared and would have expected me to manage both my son's health and my job as if nothing were wrong. But Dawn's coaching wasn't about maintaining my productivity in the face of a crisis; it was about protecting my humanity. She held space for my struggle and, in doing so, made a devastatingly difficult time a tiny bit easier. That is a ripple of loyalty and trust that no performance review or bonus could ever create. Her presence and support were the real work.

Coaching Through the Breakthrough

Inflection points aren't all setbacks. Some are upward swings:

- That moment when someone steps into a bigger, scarier role
- When a person finally believes they're ready—even if the world hasn't said so yet
- When a promotion brings more visibility than confidence
- When ambition kicks in and self-doubt follows closely behind

These are exciting—but, make no mistake, they're still disruptions. And people often don't know how to metabolize success.

The coaching shift here is subtle: less reassurance, more reflection. Try asking:

- "What do you want to prove to yourself in this next chapter?"
- "What might change about how you lead, now that others look to you differently?"
- "What muscle do you need to build to own this space, not just occupy it?"

One of my team members once said, after a promotion, "I keep waiting for someone to tell me I'm doing it wrong."

I responded, "No one's going to tell you—you have to tell yourself what great looks like now. And we'll co-create that vision, together."

When you coach someone through success, your job is to help them catch up to their own becoming.

Tools and Touchpoints for the Turning Point

Let's make this practical. Coaching through inflection points requires more than intuition—it needs rhythm, reflection, and readiness.

Here are a few habits I've found powerful:

Inflection Point Playbook: Coaching Through a Career Breakthrough or Breakdown

For a Breakthrough (e.g., a big promotion):

Acknowledge the Identity Shift: The first coaching conversation shouldn't be about tasks. It should be about identity. Ask: "This is a fantastic achievement. Who do you want to be as a leader in this new role?"

Co-create a 90-Day Learning Plan: Focus on the two to three new capabilities they need to build. Frame it as an exciting challenge, not a list of deficits.

Identify a "Safe Sounding Board": Connect them with a mentor outside their direct reporting line where they can be vulnerable and ask "dumb" questions.

For a Breakdown (e.g., a project failure or demotion):

Hold Space Before Problem-Solving: Your first job is to listen. Let them process the emotion without immediately jumping to solutions. Use simple, empathetic phrases like, "This sounds incredibly difficult."

Separate Identity from Outcome: Gently help them distinguish between the event and their inherent worth. Ask: "This project didn't succeed, but what strengths did you demonstrate in the process that you're proud of?"

Focus on the Next Small Step: The future can feel overwhelming. Coach them to identify one small, achievable action they can take in the next 48 hours to regain a sense of agency.

Rhythms That Hold

- Schedule "re-centering" 1:1s after major career shifts (no agenda—just a check-in on energy, clarity, and confidence).
- Use voice memos or short Looms to send reminders like "You've got this—and if you don't feel like it today, that's okay too."

Questions That Ground

- "What part of yourself feels challenged right now?"
- "If you trusted your instincts here, what would you do?"
- "What support do you need to move forward with confidence?"

When You're the One at the Inflection Point

Let's be honest: Leaders hit these moments too.

Maybe it's the quarter when nothing lands.

Maybe you're guiding others while quietly rethinking your own purpose.

Maybe you just feel…off.

Coaching others through their inflection points doesn't mean you're immune to your own. In fact, the best coaches are the ones who are self-coached enough to notice when they need recalibration.

My Ask for You: When that moment comes, don't just power through. Pause. Reflect. Seek out your own coach—or even your own team. You might be surprised what comes back when you model vulnerability.

Because the most powerful coaching cultures aren't built by those with answers. They're built by leaders who remember they're still growing, too.

Where the Real Growth Lives

Inflection points aren't pauses on the path. They are the path.

Where identity is redefined.

Where resilience is rehearsed.

Where courage becomes kinetic.

As a coach, your job isn't to reroute someone around those moments. It's to walk beside them through it. To hold space without shrinking the challenge. To help them see that growth isn't about rising above discomfort—it's about rising through it.

Because coaching isn't a service we offer. It's a presence we embody. Especially when everything's changing.

The Ripple from This Chapter: The ripple from this chapter is one of resilience. When you coach someone effectively through a personal inflection point, the impact extends far beyond that individual. They feel seen and supported, which deepens their loyalty. They learn to navigate change, which they model for their peers. But what happens when these individual ripples of resilience and loyalty start to combine? They create a powerful current that can change an entire organization.

Your Coaching Action Plan: Try This Today

You've learned that a coaching leader doesn't shy away from inflection points—they lean into them. Here are five practical actions you can take today to support your team through both breakthroughs and breakdowns.

- **Listen for the Shift.** Pay close attention in your next team meeting or one-on-one. Is there a team member who is unusually quiet, seems to be second-guessing themselves, or is overly focused on external validation? Take note, and schedule a dedicated time to check in with them.
- **Hold Space Before Problem-Solving.** The next time a team member comes to you with a personal or professional challenge, resist the urge to immediately jump to solutions. Start by simply listening. Use a phrase like, "This sounds incredibly difficult. Tell me more about what's going on."
- **Separate Identity from Outcome.** When a team member experiences a setback, help them distinguish between the event and their inherent worth. Ask a question like, "This project didn't succeed, but what strengths did you demonstrate in the process that you're proud of?"
- **Coach Through a Breakthrough.** Think of a team member who has recently achieved a big win or been promoted. Don't just celebrate; coach them through the identity shift. Ask, "This is a fantastic achievement. Who do you want to be as a leader in this new role?"
- **Model Vulnerability.** When you find yourself in your own personal or professional inflection point, don't just "power through." Share your struggle and how you are navigating it with your team. This models the courage to be human and builds immense trust.

CHAPTER 8

The Power and Impact of Coaching—The Ripple Effect in Action

In the previous chapter, we focused on the deeply personal impact of coaching during critical moments. Now, we zoom out. This chapter delves into how those individual positive impacts cascade outwards, creating a self-sustaining cycle of growth that reshapes the entire enterprise, often in surprising and profound ways. We will see the ripple effect in action.

The impact of coaching doesn't stop with the initial conversation or the immediate recipient. When someone experiences the positive effects of being coached—increased confidence, clarity, feeling valued and supported—it often inspires them to offer similar support to others. It's a "pay it forward" concept, where benefits spread and multiply, creating a chain reaction.

At a Trail Blazers game, young Natalie Gilbert's nerves overwhelmed her as she stepped forward to sing the National Anthem, causing her to forget the words. In that moment of vulnerability, Coach Maurice Cheeks didn't just observe; he acted with extraordinary empathy. Stepping beside her, he placed a reassuring arm around her shoulder and began to sing, his voice a steady anchor for her rising panic. His simple, human gesture wasn't about basketball strategy or team wins; it was a powerful acknowledgment of her distress and a quiet offering of support.

In that shared moment, a palpable shift occurred. Natalie, finding courage in his presence and the sound of his voice, began to sing along, her voice regaining strength with each word. The crowd, initially hushed with concern, erupted in an overwhelming wave of applause, a testament to the beauty of human connection and kindness in action. For Natalie, it was a moment of being seen and supported when she felt most exposed, an experience likely etched in her memory forever.

Coach Cheeks' action resonated deeply with countless witnesses. It was a vivid demonstration that leadership transcends titles and game plans; it's about empathy, connection, and the willingness to offer support in moments of vulnerability. His selfless act became a powerful symbol of compassion, inspiring others to consider how they, too, could offer similar support in their own spheres of influence, creating a ripple effect of kindness that extended far beyond the basketball court. It underscored that true impact often lies not in grand gestures but in simple, human acts of empathy that make others feel seen, supported, and empowered.

When people have been coached effectively, they are more likely to mentor junior colleagues, offer constructive feedback, practice active listening, ask powerful questions, and create a supportive environment. This "paying it forward" culture leads to long-term benefits like self-sustaining growth, stronger internal networks, enhanced knowledge sharing, increased organizational agility, and a more positive and collaborative culture.

A Personal Story of the Ripple Effect: From HR Admin to Director

One of my proudest coaching success stories involves a talented employee who started as a benefits administrator. Early in our working relationship, I quickly recognized her as driven and very smart (and as a bonus, she was hilarious)). She was working on a complex implementation project for a new benefits program while also helping employees with their benefits.

Recognizing her potential, I encouraged her to expand into broader HR duties. She soon took the lead on open enrollment meetings and, as her capacity allowed, began taking on more projects. One day, she approached me about applying for a new role outside of HR, within the company. This would be a completely new position and a great opportunity for business experience. While the timing was far from ideal for my team—we were short-staffed—I wholeheartedly supported her aspirations. I reached out to the hiring manager, shared my support, and spoke to my positive experience having her on my team. Soon, she landed the new role.

Fortunately, in her new role, she and I still collaborated on some projects. While I initially thought this marked the end of her HR journey with me, she later returned to my team in a more strategic role as an HR Business Partner. She excelled in this new capacity and even opted to pursue her Master's degree at the University of Southern California. As I mentioned, she was a driven go-getter and well-respected within the organization.

She and I connected regularly on how she wanted to grow and develop. I actively looked for opportunities to give her visibility and leadership experience. For her, it was important to provide those opportunities to continue to grow and develop, which also meant I was giving her feedback on her projects and areas where she was still developing. As with everyone, she had some demands at home; she is a mother to three children, and eventually, she needed to scale back her work a bit. So, we talked about it. We moved her back into an individual contributor role and scaled back on the projects she was working on. This was also a discussion where she needed to know that taking a break was okay. We agreed that she would let me know when or if she was ready to take on more responsibility. Of course, she did, and as of writing this, she is a very successful Director leading a global team. This is the ripple effect in action—tailored coaching fostering long-term growth and success.

The Ripple Beyond the Walls: A Story of Mentorship and the "Good Leaver"

The ripple effect of a great coaching leader doesn't always stay within the company's walls. Sometimes, its most significant impact is felt long after a person has moved on to their next role, creating a lasting network of mentorship and support. My friendship and professional relationship with a leader named Eric is a testament to this enduring influence.

I met Eric after the company I was working for acquired the organization where he was a leader. He came into our organization as a VP, and we worked closely together during the integration. It was immediately clear that he was a very driven and capable leader. He managed his team through the immense change of an acquisition with grace and effectiveness; his team felt supported, the change was managed well, and he was well-liked by all who worked with him.

After a few years, however, it became clear that our organization didn't have the specific growth opportunity that a person with his drive was looking for. He made the difficult decision to leave and has since gone on to become the EVP and Executive Managing Director of North America for a global software company.

But this isn't a story of a difficult departure; it's the story of a "good leaver." It's an example of what happens when a great leader's time with a company concludes, but their impact continues. The lessons that can be learned from Eric's journey are central to the coaching mindset.

First, Eric is a mentor at heart. His desire to coach and develop people isn't a switch he turns on at the office; it is core to who he is. Years after we stopped working together, he has continued to be a source of guidance for me in my own career. In a perfect example of his generous spirit, he even took the time to chat with my son, a recent college graduate, to offer advice on how to stand out in his own career. This is the coaching ripple in its purest form—a genuine desire to help others grow, regardless of reporting lines or shared company logos.

Second, Eric embodies the powerful combination of clear drive with undeniable authenticity. His focus and ambition are transparent, but so is his character. This blend is what allowed him to lead his team so effectively during the uncertainty of an acquisition, and it's what makes his mentorship so valuable today. He proves that you can be highly ambitious while also being a genuine, supportive, and authentic leader.

Eric's story proves that when you lead with a coaching mindset, you don't just build effective teams; you build lasting relationships. The ripples of your mentorship and authenticity extend far beyond your tenure, creating a network of support and influence that continues to give back for years to come.

Organizational Impact: The Widespread Benefits of a Coaching Culture

When coaching principles are integrated throughout an organization, the benefits expand dramatically. A coaching culture leads to:

- **Improved Employee Performance and Productivity.**
- **Increased Employee Retention:** When people feel valued and supported, they're more likely to stick around. Organizations with

formal coaching programs experience **22** percent **higher retention rates**, and those that actively offer coaching see a **28** percent **reduction** in employee turnover rates. Investing in structured leadership development, often incorporating coaching, can lead to a **25** percent **reduction** in turnover. For an organization with 500 employees, a **30** percent **improvement in retention** can translate to an estimated **$1 million annually** in reduced hiring and onboarding costs alone.

Stronger Leadership Pipeline.

- **Faster Adaptation to Change:** When an organization embraces learning and development, it's better equipped to handle new challenges. Strong coaching cultures enhance team agility by **18** percent and significantly improve strategic planning capabilities by **32** percent. This is an investment in future-readiness.
- **Enhanced Innovation and Creativity:** When people feel empowered, they're more likely to share new ideas and find creative solutions. Companies that foster a strong coaching culture demonstrate a **21** percent **increase** in team innovation.

From the HR Deck: The Hidden Power of the Succession Plan
To a manager, a succession plan can feel like a bit of a morbid exercise—thinking about who would replace you if you were suddenly beamed up by aliens. But from my seat in HR, the succession plan is one of the most honest and revealing documents in the entire company. It's not just a list of names; it's a report card on which leaders are truly building a coaching culture.

Here's a little secret: when we in HR review the succession plans, we can see the ripple effect in action. We can see which leaders are simply managing their teams and which ones are actively developing future leaders.

Some managers consistently have no one on their team listed as "ready now" for a promotion. Their bench is empty. But then there are the coaching leaders. Their teams are different. They consistently have one or two people who are ready to step up. Their bench is deep with talent.

When I see a leader who is a "talent magnet"—someone who consistently develops people who go on to bigger and better roles (even if it means leaving their team)—I know I've found a great coach. They aren't hoarding talent to make their own lives easier; they are cultivating it for the good of the entire organization.

This is the ultimate organizational impact of a coaching culture. It's not just about hitting this quarter's numbers. It's about ensuring the company has the leadership it needs to be successful five years from now. A manager who coaches creates a ripple of capability that strengthens the entire leadership pipeline, ensuring the organization's future is in good hands. That, more than anything, is the long-term, strategic ROI of coaching.

Case Study: Coca-Cola International's Transformation Through Executive Coaching

The case study of Coca-Cola International (CCI) powerfully demonstrates the tangible impact of executive coaching. Facing the goal of being the best FMCG (Fast-Moving Consumer Goods) company, CCI recognized its people were crucial and used executive coaching to enhance strategic execution.

- **Improved Communication and Collaboration:** CCI provided a standardized coaching platform across different regions, ensuring consistent training and development. This fostered clearer communication channels and a shared understanding of goals, breaking down silos and promoting collaboration among diverse teams. This led to more aligned efforts, reduced misunderstandings, and smoother workflows.
- **Higher Morale and Engagement:** By investing in employee development through coaching, CCI demonstrated a commitment to its people. This increased employee engagement and created a more positive and supportive work environment. This resulted in increased productivity and lower turnover rates.
- **Stronger Performance Culture:** Coaching helped CCI enhance its leadership capabilities, equipping leaders to inspire and guide

their teams effectively. This contributed to a stronger performance culture with a focus on continuous improvement and growth. The organization became more agile and adaptive, better equipped to respond to market changes and achieve its strategic objectives.

- **Enhanced Innovation:** Coaching empowered leaders to encourage creativity and initiative within their teams. This fostered a culture where employees felt safe sharing ideas and experimenting with new approaches. CCI saw a rise in innovation, leading to the development of more effective strategies and a competitive edge in the market.

What Coca-Cola's experience proves is that a deep investment in people doesn't just feel good—it creates a seismic shift in how a massive organization operates, from the C-suite to the frontlines.

Other compelling examples include Satya Nadella's cultural transformation at Microsoft. He implemented a coaching-oriented style emphasizing empathy, listening, and empowering employees, shifting from a competitive culture to a collaborative, learning-oriented one. This involved encouraging risk-taking, experimentation, and learning from failures, leading to renewed innovation, increased engagement, and a surge in stock price. Similarly, Frances Hesselbein's transformation of the Girl Scouts focused on empowering members and volunteers through a leadership approach emphasizing listening, collaboration, and valuing contributions. This shifted the culture to be more inclusive and member-driven, increasing membership and purpose. These cases highlight how coaching-oriented leadership can drive significant organizational change and improve performance.

The Ripple Effect Across Industries

To counter the idea that coaching is only for creative fields or corporate settings, let's examine how its principles create powerful impacts across a diverse range of industries. The fundamental need for growth, support, and effective communication is universal, and coaching provides the framework to meet that need, whether in a hospital, a trading floor, a classroom, or a tech campus.

Health care: The Ripple of Wellness at Mayo Clinic

In the health care field, physician burnout is a critical issue that impacts both staff well-being and patient care. The Mayo Clinic implemented a physician coaching program aimed at enhancing leadership skills and personal resilience. The results were profound. Coached physicians reported significantly lower rates of burnout and higher job satisfaction. This positive change extended directly to patients. As doctors honed their empathetic communication skills through coaching, patient satisfaction scores improved.

The benefits didn't stop there; nurses on the coached physicians' teams reported higher morale and a more collaborative environment, leading to a measurable decrease in staff turnover on those units. The coaching created a dual benefit: one of wellness for the physicians and one of improved care for the patients, demonstrating that human-centered leadership is a critical component of operational excellence in health care.

To further enhance the impact of coaching in health care, leaders can follow these guidelines:

Prioritize Empathy: In health care, empathy is crucial. Encourage leaders to actively listen and show genuine concern for their team's well-being. This fosters a supportive environment where staff feel valued and understood.

Promote Work–Life Balance: Health care professionals often face high levels of stress and burnout. Implement policies that promote work–life balance, such as flexible scheduling, mental health days, and access to wellness programs.

Encourage Continuous Learning: The health care field is constantly evolving. Provide opportunities for continuous learning and professional development. This not only enhances skills but also keeps staff engaged and motivated.

Foster Collaboration: Encourage a collaborative culture where team members work together to solve problems and improve patient care. This can be achieved through regular team meetings, interdisciplinary projects, and open communication channels.

Recognize and Reward: Regularly acknowledge and reward the hard work and dedication of health care professionals. This can be through formal recognition programs, bonuses, or simple gestures of appreciation.

Implement Coaching Programs: Just like the Mayo Clinic, consider implementing coaching programs aimed at enhancing leadership skills and personal resilience. This can help reduce burnout and improve job satisfaction among health care professionals.

Create Psychological Safety: Ensure that the workplace is a safe space for staff to express their thoughts and concerns without fear of judgment or retaliation. This encourages open communication and fosters trust within the team.

Adapt to Cultural Nuances: Recognize and respect the diverse cultural backgrounds of health care professionals. Adapt coaching methods to fit regional nuances and promote inclusivity.

By following these guidelines, health care organizations can create a supportive and effective environment that enhances both staff well-being and patient care. This approach highlights the importance of investing in the well-being and development of health care professionals to achieve better outcomes for both staff and patients

Finance: The Ripple Effect on Bay Street and Wall Street

When you think of a major bank, the words "warm and fuzzy" probably don't leap to mind. The world of finance is built on numbers, risk management, and compliance. It's an industry where leadership has traditionally been more about managing metrics than mentoring people. But what happens when one of the biggest players in that world decides to bet on a more human-centered approach?

TD Bank Group, one of North America's largest financial institutions, found itself at a crossroads. To thrive in a rapidly changing landscape, they recognized that their leaders needed more than just technical expertise. They needed to be coaches. The challenge was immense: How do you transform the leadership habits of over 700 people leaders, shifting their focus from just checking compliance boxes to having meaningful, developmental conversations?

Let's be real: For a busy bank manager, a coaching conversation can feel like a luxury they just don't have time for. TD's solution was to build a comprehensive coaching ecosystem that made coaching not an *additional* task but a *better way* of leading.

They invested in ICF-certified training for hundreds of leaders, creating a shared language and framework for what "good coaching" actually looks like. Crucially, they also simplified administrative and compliance burdens, which is a fancy way of saying they cleared out the bureaucratic underbrush so their leaders had more time and mental space for their people. When the COVID-19 pandemic hit, they didn't pause the initiative; they adapted it for a virtual world, proving that coaching is a powerful tool for maintaining connection, especially during a crisis.

The results were a stunning validation of the ripple effect.

The first ripple was felt by the leaders themselves, who reported feeling more inspired and empathetic. This created the next ripple, which touched the employees. Feeling more supported and valued by their coaching-focused managers, employee retention and engagement scores soared.

And the final, most powerful ripple reached the customer. Those positive, internal cultural changes translated directly into better frontline service, leading to **record-high customer experience scores.**

TD Bank Group's journey is a benchmark for how even the most traditional, numbers-driven institutions can humanize leadership while driving incredible business results. They proved that investing in a coaching culture isn't just a "nice-to-have." It's a powerful, scalable strategy that builds a more resilient, engaged, and future-ready workforce, creating positive ripples that can be felt from the call center to the C-suite.

Education: The Classroom Ripple of Instructional Coaching

Think about the last time you received vague feedback. Maybe you were told to be "more strategic" or to "demonstrate more executive presence." It's well-intentioned but ultimately frustrating advice. It's like being told to "be taller"—you're not quite sure what to do with it. For years, this was the reality for many teachers. Feedback was often broad, infrequent, and left them feeling overwhelmed rather than empowered.

However, a newer, highly effective model of instructional coaching turns that entire dynamic on its head. This approach, championed by organizations like Steplab and used in many highly successful school networks, focuses on making very small, specific, high-leverage changes that have a big impact over time. It's the coaching equivalent of a surgical strike rather than a blanket memo.

The Model: Instead of a long, formal observation, a coach might observe a teacher for just 15 minutes with a laser focus. They aren't looking for everything; they are looking for one thing. The feedback isn't, "You need to improve your classroom management." It is, "Let's work on the first three minutes of your transition from reading to math. Here is one specific technique to try."

The coach then models the new technique, and crucially, the teacher rehearses it in a low-stakes environment. This isn't about shame or judgment; it's about building muscle memory. This bite-sized cycle of observation, one precise action step, and rehearsal can repeat weekly.

The Ripple Effect in Action: This model is prized for its efficiency and its undeniable impact. The first ripple is immediate: The teacher feels empowered, not overwhelmed. They have a clear, manageable action they can take tomorrow. By breaking down the incredibly complex art of teaching into its component parts, this model allows teachers to show rapid, visible improvement in specific areas, from how they ask questions to how they give instructions.

The next ripple hits the students. When a teacher's instructions are clearer, students are less confused and more engaged. When classroom management is smoother, there is more time for learning. These small, consistent improvements in teaching practice add up to a major transformation over the course of a school year, directly benefiting the students in the room. This section would be more powerful if framed as a personal lesson. This approach worked because it taught me something essential: The most significant changes often start with the smallest, most intentional adjustments. It's a lesson I first learned in a pool, and it holds true in a classroom, too.

Tech: The Oxygen Project and Data-Driven Coaching at Google

In a classic example of data validating a human-centered approach, Google's "Project Oxygen" set out to determine what made a great manager. After analyzing vast amounts of internal data, the number one trait was not technical expertise but being a good coach. Google found that the highest-performing teams were led by managers who made time for 1:1 meetings, helped people solve problems by asking questions rather than giving answers, and took an interest in their employees' lives and careers. The cascade effect was a company-wide overhaul of management training, shifting the focus to developing these core coaching competencies. This data-driven endorsement of coaching has become central to Google's culture of innovation and empowerment, creating a lasting ripple that influences how thousands of managers lead every day.

These examples illustrate that the principles of coaching are not confined to a single sector. The ripple effect of seeing potential, providing support, and fostering growth creates tangible value everywhere.

The Ripple from This Chapter: The stories in this chapter prove that the ripple effect is not just a poetic metaphor; it's a measurable, tangible force for organizational change. We've seen how a single, well-executed coaching program can create waves of retention, wellness, and innovation that touch every part of the business ecosystem, from the frontline employee to the end customer. This ripple is a promise: that your daily efforts to coach and care for your team are generating a powerful, positive force you may never fully see, but one that is undeniably real.

From the HR Deck: The Compensation Ripple
One of the hiring strategies for many Private Equity backed firms is to hire recent college graduates. These firms give them a lot of responsibility and training so that by the end of one year with the company, they have gained significantly more experience than they might have at other organizations. However, we found that these employees were requesting a title change and/or salary increase after just six months. When they didn't receive it, they often quit and were hired elsewhere, sometimes at double their previous pay.

To address this issue, I collaborated with the VP of Engineering and Randi, who was the R&D HRBP at the time, to develop a career progression plan for these top-performing employees. This plan ensured that every six months, they received some form of recognition for their performance. By the end of two years, they had reached the professional level of our career path. This standardized process-maintained equity and provided employees with a clear understanding of what was required to achieve a promotion.

This approach also had a systemic impact on our compensation structure. By creating a clear and consistent career progression plan, we ensured that compensation adjustments were fair and transparent. This helped maintain internal equity and prevented the ripple effect of compensation disparities that can arise when employees leave for higher-paying opportunities elsewhere. In essence, our career progression plan not only retained top talent but also reinforced a culture of fairness and equity within the organization.

The ripple from this chapter is one of possibility. The stories from health care, finance, and my own career prove that this is not just a theory; it's a measurable force for organizational change. We've seen what's possible when a coaching culture takes hold. The final question is no longer "Does it work?" or "What does it look like?" The final question is, "How do I start?"

Your Coaching Action Plan: Try This Today

You've seen how coaching creates a ripple effect that spreads across an entire organization. Here are five practical actions you can take today to recognize and amplify those ripples within your own team.

- **Recognize a "Good Leaver."** Think of a talented former team member who left for a new opportunity. Send them a quick message to let them know you're still thinking of them and wish them well. This small act of connection proves that your mentorship extends beyond the walls of your company.

- **Identify a "Talent Magnet."** Observe the managers around you. Who consistently has a strong bench of talent? Who develops people who go on to bigger and better things? Take a moment to name that behavior for them, praising them for being a "talent magnet" and a great coach.
- **Launch a "Pay It Forward" Challenge.** In your next team meeting, ask everyone to commit to one small act of coaching for a peer or junior colleague before the next meeting. This could be anything from sharing a template to offering feedback. This reinforces that coaching is everyone's job.
- **Connect a Story to a Statistic.** Think about a personal story of coaching from your own career, or from this chapter. The next time you're in a meeting and someone questions the value of a "soft skill," share that story and follow it with a powerful statistic from this chapter (e.g., "This isn't just a nice story. Companies with strong coaching cultures report 47 percent higher revenue per employee").
- **Champion the Coach.** Look at your team's current development plans. Is there a team member who is an exceptional coach to their peers, but it isn't formally recognized in their performance review? Take a step today to add that competency to their plan, demonstrating that this skill is valued and rewarded.

CHAPTER 9

The Manager's Playbook for Building a Coaching Culture

We have seen the proof. We've explored the mindset, learned the skills, and witnessed the powerful impact of a coaching culture in action. This chapter is where the rubber meets the road. It is the manager's playbook, a comprehensive guide to take these ideas off the page and put them into practice with your team, starting with your very next conversation.

Part 1: The Foundation—Rebuilding Your Team's Relationship with Feedback

Throughout our schooling, from kindergarten through college, feedback is a constant presence. Yet, in the professional world, it often becomes something to be feared. The stakes feel higher, power dynamics come into play, and few of us are ever formally trained on how to give or receive it well. As a manager, your most important job in building a coaching culture is to reverse this trend. You must transform feedback from a dreaded annual event into a normal, healthy, and ongoing part of how your team operates. This journey requires an intense shift, and it starts with a simple foundation: psychological safety.

Ironically, these very factors, fear, high stakes, and power dynamics can create a perfect storm where feedback, a tool meant for growth, becomes a source of anxiety. I experienced this firsthand with a manager who, on the surface, was doing all the "right" things, even setting the expectation for weekly feedback sessions—a rhythm that should, in theory, create a great coaching dynamic.

The problem was, the foundation of trust wasn't there, she had just joined the team as the new leader when most people are anxious about what changes the new leader may make. Our conversations felt more like interrogations than developmental dialogues. And the feedback itself was often vague, personal, and completely unactionable, and candidly, it felt forced. Despite the fact that I was consistently exceeding my goals and making significant contributions to the team, the feedback I received was often a personal judgment.

I'll never forget one of these 1:1's, that I had already begun to dread, my feedback was first a question "Do you even enjoy what you do?"

I was completely taken aback. I had put so much effort into and passion into building this team and the function. We had great credibility and the company culture was positive. I had built out so many programs that I was so proud of. A robust, truly ingrained DEI program, career-pathing and leadership programs, Global Mobility... I can go on, but I loved what I did and seeing the impact of that and receiving the quick messages about how truly special the culture was. And, I told her that.

"You just don't look like you're enjoying your job, at least that is the facial expression you give."

This is why, as managers, our first job isn't just to talk but, instead, to create the safety and trust that makes real feedback possible.

I remember thinking, "Does my face not have the correct level of corporate enthusiasm today?" The comment had nothing to do with my performance, my results, or my behavior. It was a subjective interpretation based on the expression I would get when I was focused on actively listening to others on our virtual meetings, and it left me with absolutely nothing to act on. What was I supposed to do with that feedback? Practice smiling in the mirror before our next meeting?

That experience was a powerful lesson. It proved that the process of giving feedback is meaningless without the right intent and a foundation of trust. Setting a weekly cadence for feedback is just going through the motions if the content is not specific, behavioral, and genuinely aimed at helping the other person grow. Without that, you're not coaching; you're just creating a weekly appointment for someone to feel criticized and confused. It's the perfect recipe for eroding trust and making a high-performer start to wonder why they're trying so hard in the first place. I decided to own the change and I took another job.

A Case Study in Safety: When a Decorated Office Meant Everything

True leadership isn't about grand pronouncements or perfectly crafted policies. Sometimes, it's the quiet acts of observation, the deeply personal gestures, which resonate most powerfully and create that sacred space we call psychological safety. My own journey, and the incredible impact of a leader named Joy, taught me this meaningful truth.

Our story began when I walked into an interview for what would become, without exaggeration, one of the worst jobs I've ever had. Joy was part of the hiring team then, though she had already moved on by the time I started. I took that job out of sheer necessity, a difficult period where both my husband and I had been laid off. So, when that company predictably imploded, my professional confidence wasn't just shaken—it was in shatters. It was Joy who tossed me a lifeline, calling me to help with some projects at her new company. That call was the first of her ripple effects.

Despite this new opportunity, a deep-seated hesitation lingered. After two layoffs in less than two years, I was hesitant to truly settle in, even after returning from maternity leave. I remember consciously leaving my office walls bare, avoiding bringing in anything personal. Having to pack up another box of my stuff after yet another unexpected departure? The thought alone was unbearable. My office wasn't just my workspace; it was a physical monument to my fear.

And this, my friends, is where Joy's leadership became utterly, beautifully human. She and the team noticed the bare walls in my office. Without me saying a single word, they just got it. They understood that my bare walls were basically screaming my unspoken fear. So, what did they do? They took matters into their own hands and decorated it for me. They hung up my pictures and literally made the space feel "lived in." That simple, tangible act wasn't just thoughtful; it was one of the most powerful coaching moments of my entire career. It was a nonverbal signal that echoed, "We want you here. We want you to stay. You are safe." That tangible act was exactly the trust I needed to finally shake off my fear and truly dive into the role and the team. Joy's actions were a masterclass in the foundational element of any coaching culture: promoting psychological safety.

From the HR Deck: The Manager as the First Responder
From my seat in HR, I have a unique view of the entire organization.
I see the data, I help write the policies, and I'm involved in the most
sensitive employee situations. And in all my years of experience, one
truth has become crystal clear: HR is not the first line of defense. The
manager is.

You, the manager, are the organization's "first responder." A man-
ager who can have a real coaching conversation with a struggling
employee can solve a problem weeks or even months before it ever
needs to be escalated to HR. A manager who builds psychological
safety creates a team that is resilient and self-sufficient. This is why
building a coaching culture is so critical. It's about empowering you,
the manager, to be the most effective first responder possible.

Part 2: The Framework—Seven Steps to Fostering a Feedback Culture

Building on that foundation of safety, here are seven actionable steps you, as a manager, can take to create a thriving coaching culture within your team.

1. Promote Psychological Safety: This is the bedrock. You must create an environment where your team members feel safe to take risks, voice their opinions, and acknowledge mistakes without fear of punishment. Think of it as creating a "no-judgment zone." Model vulnerability by admitting your own mistakes—after all, nobody's perfect! Run "blameless postmortems" when things go wrong, focusing on "what can we learn?" and not on "whose fault is it?" Remember, it's about learning, not blaming.

2. Cultivate a Growth Mindset: Encourage your team to view challenges and feedback as opportunities to learn, rather than as judgments on their worth. Praise effort, persistence, and the learning process, not just successful outcomes. Normalize the phrase "I haven't mastered that yet"—because, let's face it, we're all works in progress. Think of it as turning "failures" into "epic learning adventures."

3. Provide Training: Don't assume your team knows how to give or receive feedback well. Coach them on it. Introduce simple frameworks like the SBI (Situation–Behavior–Impact) model.

This is the business equivalent of Coach Zirzow pushing me to refine my swimming technique , or Coach Summitt teaching her players the "Definite Dozen" principles; it's about breaking down a complex skill into learnable actions. Role-play difficult conversations in a safe environment. It's like practicing for a play—the more you rehearse, the better you'll perform when the curtain goes up.

1. Encourage Ongoing Feedback: Shift away from the dreaded annual review and make feedback a continuous, informal conversation. Use the 1:1 agenda template from the toolkit. Conduct brief debriefs after major projects. Think of it as a never-ending feedback fiesta—the more, the merrier!

2. Emphasize Two-Way Communication: Make it clear that feedback is a dialogue, not a monologue. Explicitly ask for feedback on your own performance. Use coaching questions to help your team members reflect on their own work, rather than just telling them what you think. It's like a game of Ping-Pong—the conversation should go back and forth.

3. Recognize and Reward Growth: Acknowledge and celebrate team members who actively seek out and apply feedback to improve. Offer simple verbal praise. Link a demonstrated commitment to growth with opportunities for more challenging and visible assignments. Think of it as giving out gold stars—everyone loves a little recognition!

4. Lead by Example: This is the most important step. Your team is far more likely to embrace feedback if they see you doing the same. Think of it as a feedback dance party—you can't expect them to boogie if you're not on the dance floor! Actively request feedback from your team, listen without defensiveness (no dance-offs here), and then visibly demonstrate that you are acting on it. Show them that feedback is the rhythm to your groove

From the HR Deck: Empowering the Next Wave of Leaders
One of my core beliefs as a leader is that the most powerful improve-
ments don't come from the top down—they come from the people
closest to the work. I was known for not just asking for my team's
recommendations but for giving them the authority and support to
act on them.

I remember when my team brought up a key pain point: hiring
managers weren't consistently performing the key steps to ensure a great
candidate experience. The process felt disjointed, and the candidate's
journey from offer to onboarding was inconsistent. Instead of taking
on the project myself, I told them, "Great suggestion! How would you
like to take the lead on building that out?"

They took the initiative and ran with it, building out a manager
"Just In Time" checklist. This comprehensive tool had tasks from the
moment a candidate accepted an offer to well into their onboarding.
They trained managers on how to use it, turning a chaotic process into
a structured, welcoming, and positive experience for each new hire.
This made it look like we had our act together from the outside, even
when it didn't always feel that way on our end.

The ripple effect was immediate and meaningful. Not only did
my team solve a critical business problem, but they gained invaluable
leadership experience and visibility. Their confidence soared, their
peers saw a new model for taking initiative, and the entire team un-
derstood that their ideas were not just heard—they were trusted. That
is the essence of a coaching culture: you don't just develop people in
theory, you empower them to lead in practice.

Part 3: The Example of What Not to Do—Learning from a Toxic Culture

To truly understand what a coaching culture is, it's just as important to understand what it is not. A toxic, micromanaging culture is the direct antithesis of everything we've discussed.

It's the opposite of Andy Reid's player-centric, empowering approach; it's a culture built on control rather than trust, much like the rigid, unforgiving atmosphere that Bill Belichick was known for at times. You know the drill—if your manager knows what brand of staples you're using, and precisely how many, you might be living this nightmare.

I recall a time when our CPO exited the company, and our leadership team was left without a head for what felt like an eternity. For eight long months, we were adrift, a group of experienced VPs operating without a rudder, a situation that ironically cultivated a great deal of trust and teamwork. But that all changed with the arrival of our new Chief People Officer. The microscope we found ourselves under wasn't just a new reality; it was a total eclipse of professional autonomy.

She was infamous for rewriting our communications, seemingly convinced she was the sole competent soul capable of such tasks. It felt like a constant barrage of "gotcha" moments—if anything happened without her express, prior approval, we were immediately contacted via chat or a tense phone call. I learned this the hard way when one of my team members publicly shared recognition for an employee. The praise, which was truly impressive, had come from an executive who had recently left the organization. Our team had a goal of giving every member recognition, and this was an employee who had not yet received any. It wasn't the employee's fault that the executive was no longer with the company, but to our new CPO, the lack of control was an unforgivable offense. The meeting was accompanied by rapid-fire Teams messages, and as soon as it was over, an immediate call to berate me. This disregard for boundaries extended well beyond office hours. On Father's Day, while I was hosting my parents for dinner, she insisted I get on a call with her. I had to excuse myself from my family to review a spreadsheet that she had questions about, a perfect example of her belief that her needs superseded any personal commitments.

My team was close-knit and we leaned on each other for support, sharing bewildered glances on Zoom and finding humor in the absurdity of it all (mostly because if we didn't laugh, we'd cry). We joked about needing a "staples report" detailing how many we'd used and why, a dark comedy born from the constant scrutiny. In the end, the environment became unsustainable, and I did exit the company, as did other valuable talent. This experience vividly underscored that micromanagement doesn't just frustrate; it erodes trust, stifles initiative, and can drive away valuable talent.

This experience vividly underscored a destructive pattern that goes beyond simple management style; it's a mindset that becomes its own self-fulfilling prophecy.

The Premise of Incompetence: The micromanager starts with the assumption that their team is incapable.

The Response of Control: Because they don't trust their team, they strip away autonomy.

The Team's Reaction: Faced with a total of lack of trust, the team naturally disengages. Why take initiative when your work will be redone anyway?

The Prophecy Fulfilled: Inevitably, a perceived failure occurs. This event becomes the "proof" the manager was looking for, reinforcing their need for even tighter control.

The good news is that these systems are not permanent. Organizations can reverse these toxic effects, but it requires intentional, courageous, and consistent effort. This begins with three critical shifts: shifting leadership behaviors, implementing continuous constructive feedback, and aggressively rebuilding psychological safety.

Beyond micromanagement and narcissistic leadership, here are several other common toxic management styles:

The Bully Boss

This manager uses their position of power to *intimidate, demean, and control* others. They create a culture of fear, where employees are afraid to speak up, take risks, or voice honest feedback. Bully bosses may use shouting, public humiliation, or threats to get what they want, leading to high employee turnover and a demoralized team.

What can you do? Focus on staying calm and professional. Document everything: save e-mails, meeting notes, and any instances of their behavior. When possible, communicate with them in writing so you have a record. If the behavior violates company policy or a law, report it to HR or a trusted senior leader, providing your documented evidence. If it is purely a difficult personality, continue to be professional and focus on your work, knowing that their behavior reflects on them, not on you.

The Ghost (or Absentee) Manager

This is a manager who is physically or emotionally *unavailable*. They fail to provide guidance, feedback, or support and often delegate important decisions to their team without providing clear direction or resources. This style can leave employees feeling abandoned, unsupported, and unsure of their priorities, leading to decreased productivity and engagement.

What can you do? Take the initiative to create a system that works for you. Schedule **regular check-ins** (e.g., a 15-minute weekly meeting) to get clarity on priorities and to update them on your progress. Prepare an agenda in advance to keep the meeting focused. If they're unresponsive to your requests, keep a record of your attempts to communicate. This demonstrates your proactive effort and can be used to show a need for better support.

The Credit Grabber

This manager takes *personal credit for the team's successes* while shifting blame onto others for any failures. They create an environment where collaboration is stifled, as employees feel their hard work will not be recognized. This toxic behavior erodes morale and trust, making the team hesitant to innovate or contribute new ideas.

What can you do? Protect your work by being strategic about communication. **Send summary e-mails** after a project is completed, clearly outlining your contributions and the team's successes. CC relevant stakeholders or team members. This creates a public, written record of your involvement. During team meetings, use phrases like, "I'm excited about the results we got from the initiative **I led**," or "My analysis showed…" This subtly but clearly links you to the work.

The Perfectionist

This manager sets *unrealistic and impossible standards*, expecting every task to be completed flawlessly. They are often unable to delegate effectively because they believe no one can do the job as well as they can. This behavior leads to wasted time and effort, as employees endlessly rework projects to meet the manager's unattainable expectations, resulting in burnout and a lack of job satisfaction.

What can you do? Instead of trying to meet impossible standards, focus on managing their expectations. Before you begin a task, **clarify the desired outcome** and the acceptable level of detail. Present a plan with milestones and get their approval. When you're ready to submit, explain your process and the decisions you made. If they demand excessive revisions, politely ask for clarification on the specific goals of the changes, showing that you are working to meet a clear objective rather than just performing endless busywork.

The Pushover

On the opposite end of the spectrum, the pushover manager is *overly concerned with being liked* and avoids conflict at all costs. They fail to hold employees accountable for poor performance, enforce deadlines, or make difficult decisions. This creates a chaotic and unproductive environment where high-performing employees become resentful and disengaged, as they see a lack of accountability and fairness.

What can you do? Since they avoid making decisions, you'll need to step up and provide the structure. **Be proactive** in outlining deadlines and roles within your team. For a team member who isn't performing, schedule a private conversation to discuss expectations. Then, document the conversation and send a follow-up e-mail. If the issue persists, present the situation and a proposed solution to your manager, making it easy for them to agree and take action. Frame the problem as a team efficiency issue, not a personal one.

What If It's Me?

If you recognize some of these toxic traits in yourself, take a deep breath. The fact that you're even asking this question means you're already on the right track—and frankly, your team is lucky you picked up this book. These aren't permanent personality flaws; they're simply habits, and like any bad habit (say, binge-watching reality TV), they can be broken with a little effort and self-awareness.

Here's how to begin breaking free from these habits:

For the Bully Boss

Let's be real, a little aggression might feel good in the moment, but it's about as effective for long-term results as yelling at your smart speaker to turn off the lights. It doesn't work. Your behavior may stem from a place of insecurity or a belief that a clenched fist gets things done. Recognize that fear doesn't inspire loyalty or great work; it just makes people update their resumes. Start by actively practicing empathy. Before reacting, ask yourself: "How will my words impact this person? What's the best way to get what I need without turning into a fire-breathing dragon?" When you feel the urge to lash out, take a moment to breathe and reframe your feedback in a constructive, private way. Focus on the problem, not the person.

For the Ghost Manager

You might think you're giving your team space, but to them, you're the leader who's permanently on a coffee break. Your absence might be a result of a heavy workload or a misconception that you're a hands-off guru. Understand that your team needs structure and support to thrive; they aren't mind readers. Make a commitment to regular, brief check-ins. Put them on your calendar and treat them as nonnegotiable. By showing up and providing consistent support, you'll stop being the phantom of the office and become a real, live leader who builds trust and helps their team feel valued.

For the Credit Grabber

This habit is the workplace equivalent of taking a team project and slapping a giant "I DID THIS" sticker on it. It often comes from a deep-seated need to be seen as successful. Remember that a truly great leader gets more credit by celebrating others than by taking it all for themselves. Practice celebrating your team publicly. Make it a point to specifically mention individual contributions in meetings, e-mails, and to your own superiors. A phrase as simple as, "This success was a direct result of Alex's excellent work on the data analysis," can make a world of difference. Your credibility will grow far more from your ability to empower others than from any personal accolades. Your success will be evident by how your team is doing, and, if you are taking the credit, they won't feel nearly as inspired to do great things as they will if you give them credit for their work. Think about it this way: Simone Biles' coach, Cécile Canqueteau-Landi, didn't step up to the podium to claim the gold medal. We all know Simone won it, because that's the way it's supposed to work. It would be weird for the coach to take credit for her athlete's win, right?

For the Perfectionist

Your drive for perfection is like a soccer manager who refuses to trust his star striker to take a shot unless the setup is absolutely flawless. It can lead to a few moments of brilliance, but it also sucks the energy out of the game and makes you the bottleneck for every attack. Realize that "good enough" is often just what's needed to score. Practice delegating with a mindset of trust. Give a player like Manchester United's Marcus Rashford the autonomy to find his own shot, even if it's not the exact one you would've chosen. Learn to let go and accept that a good result achieved by the soccer team is a greater win than a perfect one achieved by you alone.

For the Pushover

You're a leader, not a doormat. Your habit of avoiding conflict likely comes from a desire to be everyone's best friend. But great leaders aren't always the most popular ones; they're the ones who inspire respect. Think of it like a championship coach: They have to make tough decisions and hold their players accountable to the team's standards, not just be their buddy.

Understand that your main job isn't to be liked but to be a leader who ensures the team's health and performance. Start by practicing having uncomfortable conversations. It can be as simple as setting a firm deadline and following through on it. When a team member underperforms, address it directly but kindly. By holding people accountable, you're not being mean—you're showing respect for your high-performing employees and building a fairer, more functional environment for everyone.

Part 4: The Tough Realities—When the Ripple Hits a Wall

While the power of a coaching culture is immense, it's crucial to acknowledge a tough reality: Not every coaching journey ends with a triumphant success story. Sometimes, despite our best efforts, a team member may not be open to coaching, or their alignment with the company's culture, values, or priorities simply isn't there. This can lead to difficult, yet sometimes necessary, decisions.

Making this call is not a failure of your coaching. It is often a recognition of one of these truths:

It's a Recognition of Misalignment: A difficult departure is often a final acknowledgment that there is a fundamental mismatch that no amount of coaching can bridge.

Your Responsibility is to the Entire Team: Allowing persistent underperformance or cultural misalignment to linger can have a detrimental ripple effect on your other team members.

A Healthy Separation Can Be an Act of Kindness: In many cases, a professional and empathetic separation is ultimately healthier for both parties. It allows the individual to find an environment where their unique skills and style can be truly valued and where they can thrive.

Handling a difficult exit with dignity creates a crucial, if somber, ripple. It sends a message to the rest of your team that while performance is expected, people will be treated with respect even when things don't work out.

Part 5: The Coach's Resilience: Sustaining Your Own Spark

We've talked a lot about pouring into others, about seeing their potential and helping them grow. But let's be real: Even the most well-intentioned coach can run on fumes. To maintain your effectiveness and prevent burnout, cultivating your own resilience is nonnegotiable. This isn't selfish; it's strategic. Because a burned-out coach creates stagnant waters.

How you experience this emotional drain and how you recharge often connects to your own personality. As an INFJ, I know firsthand the subtle art of absorbing everyone else's energy until my own well feels a bit dry. For me, quiet reflection is a must. But for my more extroverted ENFP colleague, the same work might drain them of their creative spark, requiring them to recharge by connecting with new ideas or passionate people outside of work. An ISTJ leader, who thrives on order and process, might find the constant emotional ambiguity of coaching exhausting and need to recharge by tackling a tangible, solvable project, like organizing a cluttered office or finishing a complex spreadsheet. The key is to know your own "recharge ritual."

Sustaining your spark isn't a luxury; it's the engine of your long-term impact. By prioritizing your own well-being and resilience, you ensure that your ripple effect remains strong, clear, and capable of transforming even the most challenging environments. A vibrant coach creates a vibrant culture.

The Ripple from This Chapter

The ripple from this chapter is one of conviction and possibility. The stories from health care, finance, and my own career prove that this isn't just a theory; it's a measurable force for organizational change. We've seen what's possible when a coaching culture takes hold—not just in a story but in the data and in the lives of real people. The final question is no longer "Does it work?" or "What does it look like?" The final question is, "How do I start?"

Your Coaching Action Plan: Try This Today

You've learned that a coaching culture isn't built with grand pronouncements; it's built with quiet, consistent actions. Here are five practical steps you can take today to build a foundation of psychological safety and empowerment on your team.

- **Make Your Mistakes Public.** In your next team meeting, be vulnerable and admit a mistake you recently made. Explain what you learned from it and what you are doing differently. This simple act of modeling vulnerability creates a ripple of safety for your team.

- **Run a "Blameless Postmortem."** The next time a project or process has an issue, hold a brief debrief with your team. Instead of asking, "Whose fault was it?" ask, "What can we learn from this?" and "What system or process broke down?"
- **Empower a "First Responder."** Think of a team member who is an expert in a specific process or tool. The next time a colleague comes to you with a question about that topic, redirect them by saying, "That's a great question for [Team Member's Name]. I'll let them know you're reaching out." This empowers them to lead in practice.
- **Give a "Gold Star" for Growth.** Look at your team's work from the past week. Identify someone who took on a new challenge, tried a new approach, or applied feedback to improve. Publicly praise them in a team chat or meeting, specifically linking their effort to the culture of growth you are building.
- **Ask a "Staples Report" Question.** When you feel the urge to micromanage a team member, pause. Ask yourself: "Am I trying to control this because I don't trust them?" If the answer is yes, take a step back and instead ask them, "What support do you need from me to make this a success?" This shifts your focus from control to coaching.

CHAPTER 10

The Digital Ripple— Coaching in the Age of AI

We have just assembled our complete manager's playbook, focusing on the timeless skills of coaching. Now, we turn to the most timely inflection point of our generation: the integration of Artificial Intelligence into the workplace. This chapter is the ultimate test of our coaching skills, a guide for navigating the anxiety and opportunity of AI to ensure that this new technology augments, rather than replaces, our team's humanity.

The arrival of AI isn't just a new tool; it's a new reality. From sales to finance to human resources, AI is quietly—and not so quietly—automating tasks, analyzing data, and transforming how we work. The question is no longer *if* AI will impact your team, but *how* you will coach your team through it. This chapter is your playbook for guiding your people through this new frontier, turning anxiety into curiosity and technical change into human-centered growth.

From the HR Deck: The AI Policy Ripple

The moment a sales team started using an AI tool to analyze customer calls, my phone started ringing. The legal team was concerned about privacy disclosures. The IT team was worried about data security. The sales team was worried about being "spied on." From my HR perspective, the new technology wasn't just a productivity tool; it was a massive policy and culture inflection point. My role was to bring these groups together and facilitate the creation of a new "Ethical AI" policy. We had to build the cultural infrastructure—the rules of engagement—before the technology could be truly effective. This is the HR lens: seeing the systemic human impact behind every new line of code.

Coaching Curiosity, Not Fear: The Ripple Effect of AI

Let's be honest: The arrival of AI in the workplace has been met with a mix of breathless excitement and sheer terror. The headlines are full of stories about jobs being replaced, and for many employees, AI feels less like a helpful assistant and more like the new intern who is secretly plotting to take over their desk.

As a leader, your first and most important job is to coach your team through this uncertainty. The goal is not to become a technical expert overnight, but to model and encourage a mindset of curiosity. The conversation shouldn't be, "Will this tool replace you?" It should be, "How can we use this powerful new tool to make our work more meaningful and impactful?"

I've encouraged my own teams to get curious. We've used AI to get deeper, more nuanced analysis from our engagement survey data, uncovering insights that would have taken weeks to find manually. We've used it to compare lengthy documents, like old and new versions of an employee handbook, to instantly spot the differences. A salesperson can use AI to do deeper research on leads and competitors, allowing them to walk into a meeting better prepared and more strategic.

The conversation around AI often feels like a sci-fi movie, with headlines screaming about robots taking our jobs. We've all seen the doom-and-gloom projections about AI automating everything from complex data analysis to—gulp—even basic coding. And while AI is an incredible tool capable of handling repetitive and data-heavy tasks, we need to remember something crucial: It can't run the business on its own.

Think of it this way: AI is the brilliant, super-fast race car. But who builds the car? Who tunes it, drives it, and, most importantly, teaches the next generation of drivers? That's right—people. Your entry-level staff and new college graduates are the future mechanics and racecar drivers of your organization. They bring fresh perspectives, new skills, and the foundational talent that will innovate and adapt your business for decades to come.

If we use AI as an excuse to eliminate entry-level positions, we're not just saving a few salaries; we're creating a massive talent gap for the future. You can't promote someone to lead a team if they never had the chance to be on one. We'll end up with a severe labor shortage of experienced professionals, and trust us, that's a problem AI won't be able to solve. It's like a garden where you harvest all the adult plants without planting any new seeds—eventually, you'll have nothing left.

Instead of seeing AI as a replacement, view it as a powerful copilot. Use it to automate the mundane and free up your people to focus on the human skills that AI can't replicate: creativity, critical thinking, empathy, and relationship-building. Your job as a leader is to coach your emerging talent, teaching them how to work with and leverage these new technologies. By investing in them today, you're not just being a good coach; you're building the leadership pipeline and securing your company's future.

Coaching in the AI-Integrated Workplace: Practical Examples

AI isn't just a futuristic concept; it's a tool that's already reshaping our daily work. As a coaching leader, your role is to help your team see AI not as a threat, but as a strategic partner that automates the mundane, freeing them up for the work that truly matters. Here's a look at how this plays out in different departments.

HR: From Paperwork to People

In Human Resources, the paradox is real: HR professionals are meant to be people-centric, yet they're often drowning in administrative tasks. AI changes this, but with great power comes great responsibility.

- **Before AI:** An HR manager spends hours manually screening hundreds of resumes for a single job opening, sifting through keywords and qualifications. They also spend significant time creating basic training documents and summarizing employee survey feedback.
- **With AI:** The HR manager uses an AI tool to automatically screen resumes. *This is where a word of caution is needed.* While AI can save countless hours, it's not a magic bullet. These tools can sometimes perpetuate or even amplify unintentional bias by learning from historical hiring data that may have been

discriminatory. There have already been lawsuits filed against companies for this. The key is to use the tool as a starting point, not a final decision maker. This frees up time for the HR manager to have meaningful, in-depth conversations with a wider range of candidates about their career goals and cultural fit, rather than just the ones a potentially biased algorithm selected. They also use AI to instantly summarize thousands of employee survey comments, revealing key themes that they can then use to coach leaders on improving team morale. I also have found it incredibly helpful when completing employee investigations over Teams or Meet by using the built-in AI tools to transcribe the meeting ensuring the details are captured correctly and allowing me to focus on the discussion instead of hastily writing down notes.

And let's be honest, being a cost center, many Human Resources departments are considered "lean" and there is a lot of manual work that needs to be done. If we can take back an hour spent on pulling a bunch of data together to then begin to analyze, we can spend more time on implementing programs or on the initiatives that drive the business.

- **The Coaching Advantage:** Instead of being a resume filter, the HR manager becomes a strategic coach. Their most important job is to maintain **human oversight** over the AI's output. They coach hiring managers on using AI responsibly and on the "four Cs," ensuring a focus on diverse talent and fair evaluation. The time saved on administrative tasks is reinvested in the "Connection" and "Coaching" Cs, building a more human-centered and efficient hiring process that prioritizes equity and fairness.

Finance: Beyond the Spreadsheet

The world of finance is built on data and numbers. AI can handle the "what"—the number crunching—but it's a leader's job to coach their team on the "so what."

- **Before AI:** A finance analyst spends a full day consolidating financial reports, pulling data from multiple systems into a single, massive spreadsheet. They then spend hours manually checking for discrepancies and creating a basic visualization for the quarterly business review.

- **With AI:** An AI-powered dashboard automatically pulls and consolidates data in real-time, instantly spotting anomalies and forecasting future trends. The analyst's job shifts from data entry to data storytelling. They now have the time to analyze the "why" behind the numbers and work with department heads to co-create strategic budgets.
- **The Coaching Advantage:** The finance leader coaches the team on "Critical Thinking" and "Creativity." They ask questions like, "The AI shows us where we've been. What's a crazy 'what if' scenario that the AI can't predict, and how would we prepare for it?" This transforms the finance team from a reporting function into a strategic, forward-thinking partner.

Marketing: From Content to Connection

Marketing teams are constantly creating, analyzing, and iterating. AI can be a content-generation engine, but a human coach is needed to ensure the message is authentic and connects with the audience.

- **Before AI:** A marketing specialist spends hours every week writing the first draft of social media posts, e-mail newsletters, and blog content. They then analyze campaign results by manually sifting through mountains of data to understand audience engagement.
- **With AI:** The marketing specialist uses an AI tool to generate five different draft headlines and content ideas in minutes. This allows them to spend their time refining the message with a unique human voice. AI-powered analytics instantly identify which emotional triggers or storytelling elements resonate most with their audience.
- **The Coaching Advantage:** The marketing leader coaches their team on "Connection" and "Creativity." They encourage the team to take the AI-generated starting point and add the one key

human element—the personal story, the empathetic message, or the clever insight—that the machine can't replicate. The team's focus shifts from content creation to building a genuine connection with their community.

By integrating AI thoughtfully, a coaching leader empowers their team to focus on these uniquely human skills. This is the new definition of "working smarter."

Leveraging AI to Be More Human: The Four "Cs"

Here's the paradox that I've come to believe is true: While there is a legitimate fear about losing jobs to AI, I believe that when we leverage it the right way, **we can actually become *more* human at work.**

Think about the parts of your job that drain your energy and feel repetitive—the tedious data entry, the first draft of a report, the summarizing of long meeting notes. Now, imagine if a tool could handle 80 percent of that work. What would that free you up to do?

It would free you up to double down on the uniquely human skills that AI can't replicate, what I call the four "Cs" of the human advantage. As a coach, your role is to guide your team to focus their development here:

- **Complex Problem-Solving (Critical Thinking):** AI can analyze data, but it can't navigate ambiguity or make a tough judgment call when the data are inconclusive. Your ability to tackle multifaceted challenges that require wisdom and experience becomes your superpower.
  - **Coaching Question to Ask:** *"The AI gave us the 'what'—the raw data. What's the 'so what'? What's the story this data is telling us, and what's a judgment call we need to make that the machine can't?"*
- **Connection (Empathy):** AI can simulate a conversation, but it can't build a genuine, trusting relationship with a client or a colleague. Your ability to listen, empathize, and connect on a human level is irreplaceable.

- ○ **Coaching Question to Ask:** *"That's a great email draft the AI wrote. Now, how can we add a human touch? What do we know about this client personally that can help us build a real connection here?"*
- **Creativity (Strategic Thinking):** AI can generate ideas based on existing patterns, but it can't connect disparate concepts to form a truly novel vision. Your capacity for brainstorming, strategic foresight, and "what if" thinking is where real innovation begins.
  - ○ **Coaching Question to Ask:** *"The AI generated ten solid ideas based on our past successes. That's a great starting point. Now, what's the eleventh idea? What's the crazy 'what if' idea that the AI would never think of?"*
- **Coaching (Mentorship):** AI can provide information, but it can't inspire a team member or help them navigate a career crossroads. Investing your newly freed-up time in the genuine development of your people is the most valuable work a leader can do.
  - ○ **Coaching Question to Ask:** *"Now that AI has freed up a few hours for us this week, who on the team could use some dedicated mentoring time? What's a skill we can help them develop?"*

As a leader, you can coach your team to see this potential. Try having a brainstorming session once a quarter with a simple prompt: "What is a process that feels like a time-waster, and how could we experiment with AI to make it better?" This shifts the team's mindset from passive anxiety to proactive ownership.

A Note on Ethical Use: Avoiding Tariffs on Penguins

Of course, embracing AI also means embracing responsibility. I've been taking courses and getting AI Certifications so that I can continue to be on top of my game. In fact, much of the research on the case studies for this book was done using AI. It was an incredible time-saver. However, I then fact-checked every single point to make sure what I was including was real. And yes, there were a few "facts" that the AI confidently made up.

Let's be clear: The AI isn't the problem here. It's a phenomenal tool, but it has the worldly wisdom of a supercomputer that learned about humanity by reading the entire Internet in one afternoon. It needs supervision. Our job as leaders is to be that supervisor—to encourage the team to explore, while constantly reminding them to treat its answers with a healthy dose of "trust, but verify." It's a balancing act between innovation and not ending up as the star of an embarrassing case study, like the instant classic of Michael Cohen unwittingly submitting AI-hallucinated legal cases to a judge. When you get right down to it, nobody wants their professional legacy defined by the time they let a robot convince them to put a tariff on penguins.

- **Coaching Question to Ask:** *"This is a powerful tool. What's one rule we should all agree on as a team to make sure we're using it responsibly and not just blindly trusting its output?"*

Inflection Point Playbook: Coaching Through an AI Rollout

Here is a simple, step-by-step playbook for introducing a new AI tool to your team in a way that fosters curiosity and minimizes fear.

Step 1: Announce and Anchor (The "Why" Meeting): Hold a team meeting to introduce the new tool. Spend only 20 percent of the time on the technical "how-to" and 80 percent of the time on the strategic "why."
- ○ **Your Goal:** Anchor the team in purpose, not technology. Acknowledge their anxieties openly.
- ○ **Your Key Coaching Question:** "When you see this new tool, what part makes you most nervous, and what part makes you most excited?"

Step 2: Identify Your "Curiosity Champions" In every team, there are one to two people who are naturally curious about new technology. Find them.
- ○ **Your Goal:** Create a ripple of peer-led adoption, which is always more powerful than a top-down mandate.
- ○ **Your Key Coaching Action:** Ask them to "test and teach." Say, "I'd love for you to spend some time playing

with this tool and see what you can make it do. Could you share what you learn with the team in two weeks?"

Step 3: Host "Human Skills" Huddles: Dedicate 15 minutes in your weekly team meetings to explicitly discuss the skills that AI *can't* do.

- **Your Goal:** Reinforce the value of your team's humanity to reduce the fear of being replaced.
- **Your Key Coaching Question:** "This week, where did a uniquely human skill—like empathy or creative problem-solving—make a real difference for one of our clients or projects?"

Step 4: Celebrate the "Worthy Attempts": Encourage your team to experiment. Some of those experiments will fail. That's okay.

- **Your Goal:** To create psychological safety for experimentation.
- **Your Key Coaching Action:** When an AI-assisted attempt doesn't work out perfectly, celebrate the learning. Say, "I love that you tried that. It didn't quite work, but what did we learn from it that we can apply next time?"

The Ripple from This Chapter: This chapter's ripple is a lesson in resilience. It's the quiet strength you build when you walk beside your team through their toughest moments, even when those moments involve a new technology like AI. When you coach your team through this inflection point, you foster curiosity instead of fear, setting a pattern for how your team embraces the future. You prove that even as the tools change, the core principles of human-centered leadership—our most valuable asset—remain constant and true.

Your Coaching Action Plan: Try This Today

You've learned that a coaching leader doesn't let AI replace their team's humanity—they use it to amplify it. Here are five practical steps you can take today to foster curiosity and confidence in the face of new technology.

- **Host a "Human Skills" Huddle.** Dedicate 15 minutes in your next team meeting to explicitly discuss the skills that AI can't do. Ask, "This week, where did a uniquely human skill—like empathy or creative problem-solving—make a real difference for one of our clients or projects?"
- **Identify Your "Curiosity Champion."** Find the one or two people on your team who are naturally excited by new technology. Empower them to be your early adopters by asking them to "test and teach." Say, "I'd love for you to spend some time playing with this new tool and see what you can make it do. Could you share what you learn with the team in two weeks?"
- **Celebrate the "Worthy Attempt."** Encourage your team to experiment with AI, even if the result isn't perfect. When an AI-assisted attempt doesn't work out, celebrate the learning. Say, "I love that you tried that. It didn't quite work, but what did we learn from it that we can apply next time?"
- **Frame AI as a Partner.** The next time your team needs to write a report or analyze a large data set, frame the task in a new way. Say, "Let's use AI to generate the first draft so we can focus our time and creativity on what really matters: crafting the story."
- **Co-create Ethical Rules.** The next time you introduce a new AI tool, don't just set rules—co-create them with your team. Ask, "This is a powerful tool. What's one rule we should all agree on as a team to make sure we're using it responsibly and not just blindly trusting its output?"

Conclusion: Your First, and Lasting, Ripple

As I was finalizing this book, its central theme was brought home to me in the most personal and gratifying way. I had a lovely chat with a talented woman, Jennah, I had hired on a previous team at PowerSchool. While we no longer work together, we still connect, and she remains on the team I helped build. During our conversation, she shared something that struck me deeply: Years later, people on that team still talk about me and the culture I had built there—and they talk about it positively.

It's one thing to believe in the principles of a coaching culture; it's another to hear that the ripples you started are still moving, long after you've gone. I asked her for specifics, wanting to understand what had made such a lasting impact. Her answer was a beautiful summary of everything I believe a human-centered leader should strive for.

She said the culture was built on:

- **Authenticity and a Casual Environment.** The foundation was a down-to-earth atmosphere where it was easy for people to be themselves, primarily because I was being myself. This reinforces a core truth: Your authenticity as a leader gives your team permission to show up as their whole selves.
- **Vulnerability that Creates Connection.** She recalled the rich, human, and honest conversations we had as a team, from ERG discussions and "lunch and learns" to moments when I opened up about my son's struggles. This vulnerability wasn't a weakness; it was the catalyst for genuine inclusion and connection.
- **Humor and Lightness.** We cultivated a space where it was okay to be silly and not take everything so seriously. This humor was a crucial ingredient for resilience, especially during stressful times.
- **Connection, Even When Remote.** She remembered feeling deeply connected to the team, even when many of us were

remote. We achieved this by intentionally weaving casual, non-work conversation into our meetings. It normalized the idea that we were people first, colleagues second, and that joking and chatting while discussing work was part of building a strong team.

- **Opportunities for Collaboration and Growth.** She highlighted the value of creating opportunities for people to collaborate across teams through initiatives like ERGs, our "Fusion" projects, and even "Bring Your Kid to Work Day." These were not just events; they were structured chances for people to get project exposure and build relationships outside of their immediate roles.

- **Permission to Be Human (An "Open Door" Policy).** Finally, she mentioned that my stories about team members being able to come into my office to just vent had resonated deeply. It gave others permission to be candid and honest, even if what they needed to say was "negative" or unpleasant. She reminded me that when a leader offers that space to be raw, it's the ultimate sign of trust and safety.

This feedback was a gift. It was tangible proof that the principles in this book are not just theoretical. They are the building blocks of a lasting legacy. The ripples you create through your leadership—through your authenticity, your vulnerability, and your commitment to your people—will continue to move long after you've left the room. They become the stories people tell, and they become the culture that endures.

We've journeyed from the swimming pool to the boardroom, from the fundamentals of a coaching mindset to the complexities of leading in an AI-driven world. We've seen how coaching is not a "soft skill" but a strategic imperative with a measurable return on investment. It is the engine of innovation, the foundation of resilience, and the heart of a culture where people don't just work—they thrive.

The core message of this book is simple: Your leadership creates a ripple. Through the systemic lens of an HR leader, we've explored how these ripples can be guided, especially during the critical inflection points that define our work lives.

Starting a coaching culture doesn't require a grand, top-down initiative. It starts with you. It starts with your next conversation. It starts with choosing to ask a powerful question instead of giving a quick answer. It starts with celebrating a small, incremental win. It starts with seeing the potential in someone and having the courage to reflect it back to them.

That is your first ripple. And it has the power to change everything.

Coaching Culture Cheat Sheet: Your Quick Reference Guide

For the busy leader, manager, team lead, project manager, or individual contributor looking to influence their environment, here's a condensed guide to the core principles and actionable tips from this book. Keep this handy to quickly re-center your coaching mindset and amplify your impact.

Key Coaching Mindset Principles

- **See Potential:** Believe in others' inherent abilities, even when they can't see it themselves.
- **Embrace the Ripple Effect:** Recognize that positive coaching cascades, inspiring others to pay it forward.
- **Lead with Care and Challenge:** Combine genuine personal connection with direct, honest feedback for growth.
- **Foster Growth Mindset:** View feedback and setbacks as opportunities for learning and development.
- **Prioritize Psychological Safety:** Create an environment where vulnerability and risk-taking are safe.

Essential Coaching Skills

- **Active Listening:** Truly hear and understand (not just wait to speak).
  - *Tip:* Paraphrase to confirm understanding. Ask clarifying "what" or "how" questions.
- **Powerful Questioning:** Guide discovery ("What have you tried?" "How might you approach X?").
  - *Tip:* Be comfortable with silence; let them think.

- **Empathy and Support:** Connect personally and offer partnership ("I'm here to support you").
  - *Tip:* Validate feelings, even if you don't agree with the action.
- Constructive Feedback (SBI Model): Specific, observable, impactful.
  - *Situation:* When/where it happened.
  - *Behavior:* What was observed.
  - *Impact:* The effect of the behavior.
  - *Tip:* Deliver promptly and privately.
- **Empowerment:** Delegate with intent, provide resources, not just answers.
  - *Tip:* Resist the urge to "fix it" for them.
- **Patience and Persistence:** Growth takes time. Celebrate small wins, learn from setbacks.
  - *Tip:* Consistent check-ins reinforce commitment.

Situational Coaching and Feedback Tips

- **Know Your People:** Understand individual motivators, learning styles, and communication preferences.
  - *Tip:* Ask questions like, "How do you prefer to receive feedback?" or "What helps you feel most supported?"
- Adapt for Generations:
  - **Gen X:** Clear, concise, direct feedback; frame as opportunity; respect independence.
  - **Millennials:** Regular, specific feedback; explain the "why"; link to development.
  - **Gen Z:** Real-time, transparent feedback; focus on impact/purpose; use digital tools.
- **Two-Way Feedback:** Encourage "coaching up" and actively ask for feedback on your own leadership.
  - *Tip:* Model receptivity by thanking for input and demonstrating change based on it.

Cultivating a Coaching Culture

- **Communicate the Vision:** Clearly articulate *why* coaching is essential for individual and organizational success.
- **Involve Everyone:** Engage employees in shaping the coaching approach.
- **Lead by Example:** Leaders *must* model coaching behaviors and accept feedback themselves.
- **Provide Ongoing Support:** Training, mentoring, and resources are crucial for continuous development.
- **Recognize and Celebrate:** Acknowledge and reward effective coaching and growth.
- **Measure Impact:** Track qualitative and quantitative data to show the ripple effect.
- **Be Patient and Persistent:** Cultural change is a marathon, not a sprint.
- **Integrate Systems:** Weave coaching into performance management, talent development, and so on.

Appendix: The Manager's Toolkit

Welcome to the most practical part of the book. Think of this as your "in case of emergency, break glass" kit for leadership. These are the templates, checklists, and scripts you can pull out when you're facing a new challenge and thinking, "Okay, what would a great coach actually do right now?"

These tools are designed to be simple, actionable, and to help you start creating those positive ripples from day one.

Tool 1: The Coaching 1:1 Meeting Agenda Template

The weekly 1:1 meeting can be the single most powerful coaching tool you have, or it can be a soul-crushing status update that absolutely, positively, could have been an e-mail. This template is designed to ensure your 1:1s are consistently developmental, not just operational, making every conversation a small but meaningful ripple.

A great coaching 1:1 isn't about you getting information; it's about your employee getting clarity, support, and a space to grow. This template is designed to ensure your 1:1s are consistently developmental, not just operational.

Total Time: 40 Minutes (Protect this time like it's the last cup of coffee in the office.)

Part 1: The Check-In (10 Minutes)— "Don't Be a Robot"

This is the most important part of the meeting, and it has nothing to do with work. This is where you build the human connection that makes all the tough feedback and challenging conversations possible.

Your Goal: To listen and show you care about them as a person.

How to Do It: Start with a simple, open-ended question and then actually listen to the answer.

- "How are you? What's on your mind, personally or professionally?"
- "How was your weekend? Do anything fun?"
- "What's taking up your brain space this week?"

Pro Tip: Resist the urge to immediately solve their problem about their car making a weird noise or their toddler refusing to eat anything but crackers. You are their manager, not their mechanic or a child psychologist. Just listen, nod, and say, "Wow, that sounds tough." That's it. That's the job.

Part 2: Their Agenda (15 Minutes)— "The Driver's Seat"

This is their time. By making them own this part of the agenda, you foster ownership and accountability. They learn to come prepared to discuss their own challenges and ideas, rather than waiting for you to direct the conversation.

Your Goal: To understand their priorities, challenges, and where they need your help.

How to Do It: Put the ball in their court.

- "Great, thanks for sharing. So, what are the most important things for us to talk about today?"
- "What challenges are you facing that I can help with?"
- "Where are you feeling stuck or needing a second opinion?"

Your Role: Ask powerful questions. Don't give answers.

- "What have you tried so far?"
- "What would an ideal outcome look like here?"
- "What's one thing you could do this week to move that forward?"

Part 3: My Agenda and Feedback (10 Minutes)— "The Coaching Moment"

Now it's your turn. This is your dedicated time to provide feedback, share important context, and ensure alignment. Because you've already spent 25 minutes listening, any feedback you give now will be received much more openly.

Your Goal: To provide one piece of meaningful, developmental feedback (positive or constructive).

How to Do It: Use the SBI model we discussed in Chapter 3. Be specific.

"I'd like to talk about [Situation—the project update meeting yesterday]. I was really impressed with [Behavior—how you handled that tough question from the VP]. The impact was that [Impact—it made the whole team look prepared and confident]."

"I want to touch on [Situation—the client e-mail from this morning]. I noticed [Behavior—that we promised a deadline without checking with the tech team first]. The potential impact is that [Impact—we might have to reset expectations, which can erode trust]."

Pro Tip: *Remember, feedback is a gift. Even if it's the kind of gift that's a bit awkward to receive, like a fruitcake. Your job as the giver is to make it as tasty and digestible as possible.*

Part 4: The Look Ahead (5 Minutes)— "The High-Five and the Hand-Off"

End every meeting by ensuring you both know exactly what's next. This creates clarity and reinforces your role as a supportive coach who is there to clear the path for them.

Your Goal: To ensure alignment on priorities and offer support.

How to Do It: Ask two simple questions.

"So, what are your main priorities for the coming week?"

"How can I best support you?" or "What do you need from me to be successful?"

The Final Word: The goal is for your employee to leave the meeting feeling clearer, more confident, and more supported than when they walked in—not like they just went ten rounds with their inbox.

Tool 2: Coaching Conversation Starters

Knowing you should have a coaching conversation is one thing. Actually, starting it without sounding like a corporate training video is another. These are door openers, not magic spells. The real magic happens when you stop talking and start listening.

Before You Begin: A Quick Check-In

Before you use any of these scripts, ask yourself: "Is this a safe space? Have I built enough trust for this conversation to land?" If the answer is no, your first job is to rebuild the foundation, not deliver the feedback.

Situation 1: Giving Constructive Feedback

The Goal: To be clear and kind, focusing on the behavior, not the person.

The Opener: "Hey, do you have a few minutes to chat about the presentation from this morning?"

The SBI Follow-up: "When the client asked about our Q4 projections [Situation], I noticed we didn't have the data handy [Behavior]. The impact was that it made us seem unprepared. I'm curious, what was your perspective on that moment?"

The Coaching Question: "What could we do to feel more prepared for those kinds of questions next time?"

Situation 2: Checking In on a Disengaged Employee

The Goal: To show you care and open the door for a conversation, without making accusations.

The Opener: "I've noticed you've been a bit quieter in our team meetings lately. I just wanted to check in and see how things are going."

The Follow-up (if they say "I'm fine"): "I appreciate that. The reason I ask is that I really value your perspective, and the team misses hearing it when you're quiet. Is there anything about the team dynamic or the projects we're working on that's making it harder to jump in?"

The Coaching Question: "What would need to be different for you to feel more energized at work right now?"

Situation 3: Discussing Career Growth

The Goal: To understand their aspirations and co-create a path forward.

The Opener: "You've been doing some absolutely fantastic work on the [Project Name] project, especially with [Specific Skill]. It got me thinking about your career goals."

The Follow-up: "When you think about the next year or two, what kinds of projects or skills get you most excited?"

The Coaching Question: "What's one thing we could do this quarter to help you get a bit closer to that goal?"

Situation 4: Mediating a Conflict Between Team Members

The Goal: To facilitate a conversation, not to be the judge and jury.

The Opener (to each person individually first): "I wanted to create some space for you to share your perspective on what's been going on with [the other person]. Can you walk me through your experience?"

The Opener (when you bring them together): "Thanks to both of you for being willing to talk this through. My only goal here is to help us find a better way to work together. To start, I'd love for each of you to share what you think a successful outcome from this conversation would look like."

The Coaching Question: "What is one thing you can each commit to doing differently this week to improve this dynamic?"

The Final Word: These aren't magic words. They're just door openers. The real magic happens when you stop talking and start listening. Practice them, make them your own, and don't be afraid to sound like a real person—it's your biggest strength as a coach.

Tool 3: The First 90 Days as a Coaching Leader

Starting a new management role is like trying to drink from a firehose. You're flooded with new names, new processes, and a whole lot of new expectations. It's tempting to jump in and start "fixing" things immediately to prove your worth.

Don't.

A great coach knows that the first few months aren't about proving how much you know; they're about proving how well you listen. This roadmap is designed to help you create a lasting ripple effect by building trust from day one.

Days 1–30: The Listening Tour

- **Goal:** Build trust and gather context. You can't coach a team you don't understand.
- **Why This Matters:** Your team needs to feel seen before they can be led. This phase anchors you as a human, not just a new boss.
- **Your Go-To Questions:**
  - "What do you love about your work? What parts drain your energy?"
  - "What's one thing I should know about you that's not on your resume?

Key Action: The 1:1 Deep Dive. Schedule a 1:1 with every single person on your team (and key stakeholders outside of it). This is not a status update. This is a "get to know you" session.

Your Go-To Questions:

- "What do you love about your work? What parts drain your energy?"
- "What do you think this team does really well? Where do you think we could be better?"
- "What do you need from a leader to do your best work?"

"What's one thing I should know about you that's not on your resume?"

Pro Tip: *Take copious notes. When you refer back to something they told you in this meeting a month later ("You mentioned you were interested in X, and an opportunity just came up…"), it's like a superpower. It shows you were actually listening, not just waiting for your turn to talk.*

Days 31–60: The Framing Phase

- **Goal:** Create clarity and begin introducing your coaching philosophy.
- **Why This Matters:** You're metabolizing their input into a clear, shared vision. This shows them their voices matter.
- **Key Action:** The "Here's What I've Heard" Meeting. In a team meeting, play back the themes you heard (anonymously).
- "Here's what I've heard are our biggest strengths…"
- "Here's what I've heard are our biggest challenges…"
- "Based on that, here's what I believe our focus should be for the next six months…"

Introduce a Shared Language: This is the perfect time to introduce a simple tool, like the SBI model for feedback. Frame it as, "This is a tool I've found helpful for making feedback clear and actionable. Let's all try using it."

Pro Tip: This is not the time to unveil a 72-slide PowerPoint deck outlining your grand vision for world domination. Keep it simple. You're not giving a sermon; you're starting a conversation.

Days 61–90: The Empowerment Phase

You've built trust and framed the vision. Now it's time to get out of the way.

The Goal: Foster autonomy and ownership by shifting from directing to delegating with intent.

Key Action: The First Delegation. Identify a meaningful, low-risk project and delegate it fully to a team member. This is your first real test as a coach.

How to Do It: Delegate the "What," not the "How." Be crystal clear on the desired outcome, the budget, and the deadline. Then, let them figure out how to get there.

Your Role is Coach, Not Quarterback. Schedule regular check-ins, but use them to ask questions ("What roadblocks are you hitting?"), not to give instructions ("You should e-mail Susan about that.").

The Final Word: The first 90 days set the tone for your entire tenure as a leader. If you spend it talking, you'll build a team of followers. If you spend it listening, you'll build a team of leaders.

Tool 4: The "Team Trust" Diagnostic

"Psychological safety" is a term that gets thrown around a lot in business books. It's a great concept, but what does it actually feel like? And how do you know if you have it?

Think of this tool as the "check engine light" for your team's culture. It's a quick, honest gut-check to help you move from a vague feeling to a concrete understanding of how much trust exists on your team.

Think of this tool as the "check engine light" for your team's culture. It's a quick, honest self-assessment to help you move from a vague feeling to a concrete understanding of how much trust exists on your team.

The Assessment: A Gut-Check

Read the following five statements and rate how true they are for your team on a scale of 1 (Never) to 5 (Always). Be brutally honest with yourself. No one is grading you.

- Team members openly admit their own mistakes. (1–5)
- Team members are comfortable offering dissenting opinions, even to me. (1–5)
- Team members regularly ask each other for help when they are stuck. (1–5)
- Team members give each other direct, constructive feedback. (1–5)
- When a project fails or a mistake is made, the team's first reaction is to ask "What did we learn?" not "Whose fault is it?" (1–5)

Your Score: What's the Engine Telling You?

Add up your points.

21–25: The Trust Engine is Purring. Congratulations! You've built a high-trust environment. Your job now is to be a vigilant steward of that culture. Don't get complacent. Your next step: Ask your team, "What is it about our culture that makes it safe to take risks?"

16–20: The Engine is Okay, but Making a Ticking Noise. You have a solid foundation of trust, but there are inconsistencies. People might feel safe in some situations but not others. Your next step: Identify your lowest-scoring area and make it your #1 coaching focus for the next month.

11–15: The Check Engine Light is On. There are some significant trust issues that are likely hindering your team's performance and well-being. People are probably holding back, playing it safe, and avoiding vulnerability. Your next step: It's time for a "listening tour," even if you're not new. Go back to basics and focus on building human connection.

5–10: The Engine is Smoking. Red alert. You are likely operating in a culture of fear, not a culture of coaching. Innovation is probably non-existent, and your best people are likely polishing their resumes. Your next step: This is your absolute top priority. Seek out a mentor or your own manager to discuss how to fundamentally rebuild trust from the ground up.

The Final Word: This isn't a test you can cram for. The score today is just a snapshot. Your real job as a coach is to make the small, consistent deposits of trust—by modeling vulnerability, rewarding honesty, and protecting your team—that will improve this score, one ripple at a time.

Resources and Further Reading

To dive deeper into these ideas and practices, here are some resources you might find helpful:

Bibliography

Brown, Brené. *Dare to Lead: Brave Work. Tough Conversations. Whole Hearts.* Random House, 2018.

Bungay Stanier, Michael. *The Coaching Habit: Say Less, Ask More & Change the Way You Lead Forever.* Box of Crayons Press, 2016.

Character Development & Leadership. "Pat Summitt—Respect." Accessed July 22, 2025. https://characterandleadership.com/pat-summitt-respect/.

Dweck, Carol S. *Mindset: The New Psychology of Success.* Random House, 2006.

Hacking HR. "Hacking HR." Accessed July 22, 2025. https://www.hackinghr.io/.

Ibarra, Herminia, and Anne Scoular. 2019. "The Leader as Coach." *Harvard Business Review*, November–December. https://hbr.org/2019/11/the-leader-as-coach.

International Coaching Federation. "ICF." Accessed July 22, 2025. https://coachingfederation.org/.

The Institute of Coaching, "Institute of Coaching." Accessed July 22, 2025. https://instituteofcoaching.org/.

LinkedIn Learning. "Courses on Coaching Skills for Managers." Accessed July 22, 2025. https://www.linkedin.com/learning/coaching-skills-for-managers.

Matuson, Roberta. "Is Executive Coaching Really Worth the Money?" *Forbes*, July 27, 2023. https://www.forbes.com/sites/robertamatuson/2023/07/27/is-executive-coaching-really-worth-the-money/?fbclid=IwY2xjawKrCLdleHRuA2FlbQIxMQABHq0PKuL65Ob_shJqdJ5zAGmRkQaBVrRO9kZ2VinlGWWLY-M7aTZX1n0lbyzN_aem_OUGIaWtgEI76_TAL8drT5w.

Ransbotham, Sam, Shervin Khodabandeh, David Kiron, François Candelon, Michael Chu, and Burt LaFountain. 2020. "Expanding AI's Impact with Organizational Learning." *MIT Sloan Management Review*, October 20. https://sloanreview.mit.edu/projects/expanding-ais-impact-with-organizational-learning/.

Olivero, Gerald, Denise Bane, and Richard Kopelman. "The Effect of Coaching on Productivity." *Public Personnel Management* 28, no. 4 (Winter 1999): 539–55.

Packt. "Leadership and Team Management Specialization." *Coursera.* Accessed November 18, 2025. https://www.coursera.org/specializations/packt-leadership -and-team-management.

Scott, Kim. *Radical Candor: Be a Kick-Ass Boss Without Losing Your Humanity.* St. Martin's Press, 2017.

Whitworth, Laura, Karen Kimsey-House, Henry Kimsey-House, and Phillip Sandahl. *Co-Active Coaching: Changing Business, Transforming Lives.* Davies-Black Publishing, 2007.

By checking out these resources and continuing to develop your coaching skills, you can truly champion a coaching culture in your organization and create a lasting ripple effect of positive change.

About the Author

Kim Lee, SPHR, is a strategic leader, AI strategist, and compassionate coach who builds human-centered cultures. With a career spanning executive HR leadership and a deep belief in the power of coaching to unlock human potential, she guides organizations through moments of growth and change. Her philosophy was forged on the pool deck of a high school swim team, where a coach helped her discover a strength she didn't know she had. This ignited a lifelong commitment to seeing—and developing—the best in others, a belief further strengthened by her experience as a mom who raised her children on her own.

Today, Kim applies this ethos as a consultant and AI product developer, helping leaders navigate the complexities of technology and the future of work. She is also a faculty member and panelist with HackingHR. Known for managing complex situations with emotional intelligence and delivering constructive feedback that empowers growth, Kim is dedicated to helping people become the best version of themselves.

When she's not working with leaders, you can find her cheering on her team, trying out a new recipe, or searching for the perfect bottle of wine.

Index